HOW TO COPE
SUCCESSFULLY WITH

DEPRESSION

DR TOM SMITH

Wellhouse Publishing Ltd

First published in Great Britain in 2004 by
Wellhouse Publishing Ltd
31 Middle Bourne Lane
Lower Bourne
Farnham
Surrey GU10 3NH

DISCLAIMER

The aim of this book is to provide general information only and
should not be treated as a substitute for the medical advice of
your doctor or any other health care professional. The publisher
and author is not responsible or liable for any diagnosis made by
a reader based on the contents of this book. Always consult your
doctor if you are in any way concerned about your health.

A catalogue record for this book is available from the British Library

ISBN 1 903784 14 X

Also by Dr Tom Smith in the How to Cope Successfully series:
- *Colitis*
- *Crohn's Disease*
- *Diabetes*
- *High Cholesterol*
- *Thyriod Problems*

Printed and bound in Great Britain by
Creative Print & Design Group, Middlesex UB7 0LW

Contents

Dr Tom Smith

Having graduated from Birmingham Medical School, Dr Tom Smith spent two years in hospital house positions before entering general practice, first in Birmingham and then South Ayrshire. He then became medical adviser and later medical director of a major pharmaceutical company where he organized and helped to publish clinical trials of new drugs and took the Diploma in Pharmaceutical Medicine of the Royal College of Physicians of Edinburgh. Dr Smith has been a full-time writer since 1977 with many popular medical books to his credit (including Diabetes, High Cholesterol, Depression & Thyroid Problems for Wellhouse) together with weekly medical columns in several regional newspapers. He also finds time to practice as a locum for the family doctors in his home area of Girvan, Ayrshire, South West Scotland. Tom is married with two children.

Preface

When it was suggested that I write this book, I wasn't sure I was the right person to do it. I'm not a psychiatrist. Nor am I a full-time general practitioner, having chosen to practise medicine part-time for most of my professional life. The rest of the time I write – books, conference reports, newspaper columns, radio programmes, the usual round of jobs that crop up in a medical journalist's day. I am not a pharmacologist, so I cannot claim any special expertise in the action of antidepressant drugs. However, I was for seven years involved in pharmaceutical research, and have a diploma to show for it. One of my tasks in those years was to plan and control clinical trials of new antidepressant drugs. During that time I learned how much drugs can and can't do for the average depressed person.

Nor am I afflicted with depression myself, which might put me at a disadvantage compared with other authors, who admit that their interest in the illness started with their personal experience of it.

Even more damning to my choice of depression as a subject for a book is my early experience of psychiatry, as a student and hospital house officer. When I left school, I spent the summer before going to medical school as a nurse in the geriatric ward of what was then called, without embarrassment, a 'mental hospital'. A collection of large Victorian buildings in the country, so that the patients could be hidden away from public gaze, it housed hundreds of men and women who had been forgotten. There was no pretence at treatment – there was nothing to be done for them. Pills such as barbiturates were given to keep them quiet and biddable. Most lived in a state halfway between consciousness and sleep. They did not talk to each other, far less to the nurses, who were more like warders than health professionals. They were considered 'burnt out' hopeless cases, who sat and stared, and waited for their meals and bedtimes, when oblivion could, thankfully, overtake them.

A few younger in-patients with severe depression (most of them had failed in suicide attempts) were given electroconvulsive therapy (ECT): I had the privilege of watching them convulse to order on a table, and then to care for the inevitable confusion afterwards. Worse, a treatment in vogue then was insulin coma therapy, in which injections of insulin were given to deplete the brain of glucose. That made them unconscious, and they were brought round after a determined interval (how it was determined I still don't know) by an injection of glucose. Witnessing that was also frightening: some of the patients looked, during their coma period, as if they were dead, and I was always so relieved when they woke up again. They, too, faced the next few hours in a state of confusion, which did not impress me. After a few hours they were back in the day ward, and it was difficult to say whether or not the treatment had helped raise their mood. One result was certain: none of the patients who were given the ECT or insulin treatment liked it or gave consent to it with full understanding of its possible consequences. Any patient I was asked to accompany to the ECT or insulin rooms was always frightened and unhappy beforehand.

Even at 18 years old I felt that this was wrong. I reasoned that if this were all that psychiatry could offer, I would seek some other area of medicine in which to work.

Medical school didn't do much to change this opinion. Over the five years of study, we had very few weeks of psychiatric training. We had a short series of lectures and made a few fairly unproductive visits to hospital psychiatric clinics. Amazingly, the timetable had room for only two weeks in general practice over the whole four years of clinical studies. Happily, today's medical students are now attached to a teaching general practice from their first year onwards, and work in it until they qualify. As fully a quarter of general practice consultations involve depression (in the patients, that is, not the doctors), they are obviously getting much better and more appropriate training.

Once qualified as a doctor, my feelings about psychiatry didn't improve. I became a house officer in the biggest general hospital in the West Midlands. My attitude towards people with depression became coloured by the stress of my job. Dealing with dozens of medical emergencies in casualty night after night, it was difficult enough to look after the people with heart attacks, strokes, bleeding stomach ulcers, diabetic coma or acute lung failure due to chronic bronchitis without having to look after the overdoses, too.

How we housemen and women hated dealing with the 'ODs'. They came in semi-conscious, having swallowed pills. Often we didn't know what they had swallowed, or how many of them, and whether their lives were really in danger. But we had to give them spoonfuls of medicines like ipecacuanha to make them vomit, and to pass tubes down their noses into their stomachs to wash out any undigested tablets. Once round from their ordeal, they were usually less than grateful for our ministrations. We tried to keep them in the hospital until they had at least seen a psychiatrist, but they usually signed themselves out the next day. And we would see them again, a few weeks later, with another OD.

It was only too easy to label these unfortunate people as 'selfish' and as 'time wasters' who had inflicted their problems on themselves. We didn't like them very much, and they didn't like us. There was none of the caring patient-doctor relationship that was instant and natural for the person with a heart attack or lung failure. We saw them for too short a time to do anything to relieve their real problem – depression. To be frank, we were not interested in trying to help them. The sooner they were out of our care and into the psychiatrist's, the better.

Then everything changed. I went into general practice, for the first year in the city of Birmingham, then in rural South West Scotland. It was a revelation to meet people in the surgery who had true depression and who were anxious to receive help from me, not just for a few minutes, but for the foreseeable future. These were not selfish people but people with a disease just as medical as diabetes or high blood pressure or bronchitis or liver failure. It was just that the organ that was affected was not their pancreas or their heart, their lungs or their liver, but their brain. And, for the first time, we doctors now had the means to treat it.

We had the new 'miracle' drugs, the tricyclics. They had done so well in trials in just the sort of people that I had seen as an 18-year-old, the men and women with severe depression that had been locked away as hopeless. Now it was the locks that were forgotten, not the people. 'Mental hospitals' had become 'psychiatric units', with no locked wards. There was very little, and strictly controlled, use of ECT, and insulin coma therapy had gone for good. Psychiatric hospitals were brighter places, and research into the brain had discovered the magic 'neurotransmitters' – chemicals passing from one brain cell to another that control, among other things, mood. The reasoning was that depression must be due to an imbalance of these neurotransmitters, and that drugs could be found that would redress the imbalance and restore a normal mood.

So in general practice we started to prescribe the first true antidepressants. I will go into the ways different antidepressants act on the brain's transmitters in a later chapter; it is enough for now to state that the first tricyclics were welcomed as a huge benefit. If they could do so much for those patients in hospital with severe depression, we reasoned, how much more could they do for our less badly affected patients in general practice?

As is so often the case with new drugs, they did not entirely live up to their promise. Depression in long-stay patients in psychiatric hospitals seemed to be a different disease from that met with every day in general practice. The new drugs did help, but only after they had been used for several weeks. Before that time, the side effects were evident. Understandably, people living at home, trying to get on with their working and family lives, tolerated side effects from drugs far less easily than did patients in long-stay institutions. This was especially so if they included blurred vision (so that they couldn't drive), and dry mouth, constipation and bladder problems – all common with the first antidepressants.

The other problem in general practice then was time. We had so little time for each appointment: it was common for doctors to see patients at a rate of two every 15 minutes. If you were lucky, the patient booked at the same time as you had come just for a repeat prescription or a renewal of a sick note. Then you might have more than your seven-and-a-half minutes. But even a full 15 minutes isn't enough for a reasonable discussion about depression.

In one way, therefore, the new drugs did some patients a disservice. They became a way of shortening the discussion between doctor and patient. The doctor diagnosed depression, gave out the prescription, told the patient to come back in a month, and that was that. Meanwhile, the patient was left with a feeling of being dismissed, and his or her emotional needs were left unfulfilled.

This was brought home to me, as I'm sure it was to many doctors like me, by the occasional tragedy. Depression is a serious illness that needs serious attention – just as much attention as cancer or heart disease. Because it can be just as lethal. It is commoner for young adults to die from their depression than from cancer, heart attacks and strokes put together. That's because they commit suicide when they see no alternative. Depression is the number one cause of death from illness in men and women in their twenties. Yet we doctors – and I have to admit to being one of the doctors at fault – were virtually brushing it aside as something that a regular prescription of a pill could cure. I remember the bedroom of one young woman who died from an overdose. In her bedside cabinet were three full bottles of antidepressant pills, prescribed for her over her final six months. Her doctor had no idea that she had not taken them.

I also remember one man in his early forties. He was in a new job that had entailed moving from his home district to our practice. In his previous home he had been at the centre of his small-town society. He would have to start all over again in our district, with a better job, certainly, but with new friends to make and a new home to build. Only days after his move, he began to doubt that he had done the right thing. He slipped into a deep depression, seeing no future for himself, despite all the positive encouragement given by friends and family. I spent one afternoon and evening with him, trying to help him see reason – but all he could see around him was blackness.

Because I feared what he might do, I got his permission to admit him to our local psychiatric unit, where he stayed for three days. He was given the best of treatment, but to no avail. He signed himself out against the advice of his psychiatrist, and went home. He took the first opportunity after that, with his wife out at the shops, to kill himself with his car-exhaust fumes in his garage.

I felt then, and still do, many years later, that I had failed him. The management of people with depression is not just about prescribing pills. Nor is it just about spending lots of time talking to them. We have to do much more. Everyone in the family doctor's team has to help. The family must be aware of the risks and how to help. The patients themselves must be persuaded to feel that the black cloud hanging over them can be lifted. Most of all they must understand what depression is, and be aware of all the help they can get with it.

So now you have the reason for this book. Alone, your doctors can't do all that's possible. We still don't have the time to help everyone with depression in the many ways in which we would like to. But we can put before you, in a book like this, all the help you can get. To do that, we must first help you to understand why you have depression – and that is not simple. It isn't just a reaction to sad or stressful circumstances, but neither is it entirely an inherited misery that is an inevitable consequence of your genes. It may be a mixture of both.

Then there is today's mixture of treatments, from advice on how to change one's emotions, behaviour and relationships to the use of prescription drugs. This book tries to cover them all. Much of its content is taken from the writings and studies of experts in depression, but it is liberally interspersed with my own thoughts, based on my 40 years of experience as a doctor.

In treating depression we can't follow the strict rules and guidelines that we would obey with, say, patients with diabetes, infections or heart disease. Each person with depression reacts to different treatments in different ways, and not all treatments are suitable for everyone. This book offers you choices: your doctor will no doubt want to discuss them with you. Not all the choices are available in every area, and there are so many people who need treatment for depression there may be long waiting lists for some of them. So part of this book is devoted to self-help for your depression. It is not a substitute for help from your local general practice team, but it will certainly add to your ability to overcome your darkest moments.

If that is what you need, comfort yourself that you are in good company. Winston Churchill wrote of the 'black dog' that plagued him throughout his life. He could never stand near the edge of a railway station platform because he feared that, on an impulse, he might jump in front of an oncoming train. If you recognize that feeling, then this book is for you.

Chapter One

What is Depression?

It's normal to feel low from time to time. Everyone does. When circumstances are unpleasant, such as problems at work or arguments within a family, to feel unhappy is the usual, and even correct, reaction. It may be the stimulus to put things right, and that may be the reason we have moods at all. Without feeling low we would have no drive to get better. We take action to correct it, and the lower mood soon fades.

In the same way it is normal to feel 'high', too. If things are going right, we are rewarded by feelings of pleasure, and even elation. We enjoy ourselves. During the normal routine of everyday life we are usually somewhere between the two, on an even keel, with a mood that is neither high nor low, but level.

Depression is a departure from the norm. The mood drops, out of the blue, with no apparent cause. You feel it, but find it difficult to pinpoint any preceding cause. Or you may think you know the cause, but when you try to explain it to friends or family, they are at a loss to understand.

And it lasts. Most normal mood swings last a few hours, or a day or two at most. Depression continues long after that time. If you feel low for more than a week or so, and the mood stays with you all the time, hour after hour, you are depressed.

However, depression isn't just about mood. It affects almost every aspect of your life. You find that you waken in the early hours of the morning and can't get back to sleep again. You lose your enjoyment of the everyday things you cherish, like your garden or your favourite food or television programme. You don't have the energy to do things, such as take that daily walk. You are always too tired and weary. You lose your appetite, and some weight. It's rare to gain weight when you are depressed, but for a few, who are exercising much less than normally, it may happen.

You aren't as efficient at work or in doing things around the house. You blame yourself for all the things that are going wrong around you. You can't concentrate and take normal decisions about everyday things, such as what to buy when shopping or to make for dinner. You burn the food and become untidy. Even the way you walk and stand can change, so that you look 'low and slow' to other people. And your sex life disappears, as you lose all interest in your partner.

If that isn't enough, depression doesn't come alone as a symptom: you can become anxious, irritable, agitated and mentally slow, even to the point of seeming 'retarded' to your family and friends. If it persists, and becomes more severe, eventually you may stop eating, start thinking that people are against you (paranoia) and think of suicide. I make no apology for mentioning suicide so early in this book. I presume that if you are interested enough to read it, the possibility of suicide has occurred to you.

You don't have to have all of the above symptoms to be diagnosed as depressed. But their pattern is plain: if you have had an episode of depression you will instantly recognize your particular bunch of symptoms, and you may well have experienced them all.

Yet it is rare for people to complain to their doctors that they are depressed. Often they 'somatize' their problems with a physical complaint. A common one is constipation – the bowel is slowed, too. Another is difficulty in sleeping. Most people with depression fall asleep as usual, but waken in the early hours and then can't get back to sleep. Failing to get to sleep in the first place is more a sign of anxiety than depression. If you have both anxiety and depression, then the result can be a mixture of both types of insomnia.

Interestingly, psychiatrists and general practitioners differ in their experience of patients with anxiety and depression. Studies of in-patients in psychiatric hospitals strongly suggest that depression and anxiety are two distinct illnesses, and that the two don't overlap. This is certainly not the experience of general practitioners, many of whose patients show signs of both. General practitioners also feel that they can correlate the degree of depression with that of the anxiety, so that the deeper the depression, the worse is the patient's anxiety. Of course, there are people with only depression or only anxiety, but these diagnoses are not so easily distinguished by the patients, who tend not to differentiate between them. Ask yourself if you are more depressed than anxious, or the reverse, and you will see what I mean.

This mix-up between anxiety and depression can have serious

consequences. There are drugs, for example the tricyclics, that can ease depression and make people more anxious. There are others, such as the benzodiazepines, that help to calm anxiety, but can deepen depression. If the doctor is considering prescribing both, then a lot of thought must go into the prescription, and the patient has to be followed up very closely. There is much more about prescribing for depression in a later chapter.

Suspecting Depression

What makes the family doctor suspect that a patient is presenting for the first time with acute depression? We have, broadly speaking, five main groups of patient in whom we put depression in the front line of diagnoses. Few of them use the word 'depression' when they are presenting their complaint. They are people:

- who find they are not coping with their usual routine. They can't go to work, they can't even be bothered to get out of bed. Once they have struggled to dress, they can't look after the house.
- with vague symptoms that they can't describe well, such as tiredness, loss of appetite, loss of weight, problems with sleep.
- who have turned to behaviour that isn't usual for them, such as drinking too much, taking drugs, or taking to rages and violent outbursts.
- who have caused worry to their family or friends because their relationships have changed. Families may have become frustrated with them: there may be guilt feelings on both sides, and the family may have become less than sympathetic towards them.
- who talk about committing suicide, and may have made detailed plans to do so.

On this last point, anyone who has mentioned suicide should be taken very seriously. The old wives' tale that people who threaten suicide never do it is wrong. People who talk about it are more likely to do it than people who don't. A threat of suicide is an emergency that needs immediate support from the psychiatric services.

This list of five typical ways in which depression presents is not exhaustive or exclusive. The patient who has repeated bouts of headache, backache, other muscle pains and dizzy spells may be diagnosed as having fibromyalgia or myalgic encephalopathy (well publicized as ME), but often has an underlying depression as a cause of the symptoms. Palpitations, breathlessness, nausea and excessive sweating are other signals of a hidden depression.

Many people, therefore, hide their true problem in a host of other symptoms. Why do they do this? One reason is that they may think that doctors are there to help them with physical problems, and are less experienced in mental ones. Another is that they really do have these physical symptoms. Physical problems and psychiatric problems like depression often do exist together: it is just that the patient is more consciously concerned with the physical aspect of his or her illness. Yet a third reason is that, even in this twenty-first century, people believe that there is a social stigma in having a 'mental' disorder, and they are ashamed to admit they have one. A good family doctor should be able to sift the physical from the mental symptoms and get to the heart of the illness. If that is truly depression, then there is a lot of explaining and reassuring to be done. The stigma must be removed, once and for all. If the patient continues to feel guilty, with low self-esteem, the chances of getting better are less.

Depression occurs at any age, from childhood to old age, and age can make a difference to the form it takes. For example, it's common for people to assume that depression is a natural part of old age. As we slow down and become more infirm with age, so the argument goes, our brain slows, too, and with it our mood. If that is natural, the reasoning continues, then there is nothing much we can do about it. But it isn't any more natural to become depressed in old age than it is in younger people. It is still an illness that we can try to reverse, regardless of age.

The main problem for depression in old age is that it is mistaken for dementia, a condition that is less easy to influence because it is the result of a true loss of brain capacity. It must be admitted that both illnesses start in a similar way. An older person who is difficult, stubborn, complains a lot, demands a lot of his or her family and carers, who is also forgetful, confused and living in the past is often given up as having dementia, when in fact the cause is depression. And depression can respond just as well to treatment in the elderly as in younger adults.

There are clues to the difference between depression and dementia in the old. Dementia usually comes on gradually, the loss of reasoning power (cognition) is steady and present all the time, it steadily and noticeably progresses and does not improve with treatment. Yet the patient with dementia is not unduly distressed by this deterioration and retains a self-respect that is lost to the person with depression. Older people with depression have times when they are lucid and just as intelligent as they were, will respond to antidepressant measures (to be detailed in later chapters), are usually distressed by their state of mind and have a very poor image of themselves.

Children can be depressed, too. They are usually also anxious, have difficulty sleeping, are irritable, refuse to eat, won't go to school, have phobias, complain of stomach pains, become obsessive about small things, are always complaining they feel ill (a true form of hypochondria) and may even think of suicide. Children showing some or all of these characteristics are in serious danger of self-harm. There is also a very high chance that they have been sexually abused.

Teenagers are possibly the most vulnerable age group of all. We tend to expect teenagers to have emotional problems, so that too little may be made of their misery. It's common for them to be told to grow up, as if that could help in any way. Yet they are beset by self-doubt and their acceptance by their peers. They are often at odds with their parents, and are not yet mature enough to come to terms with their feelings. They are at high risk of suicide. Depressed teenagers present with just the same set of physical and mental symptoms as adults. They should be cared for especially well if they are to come through this turbulent period in their lives unscathed.

Types of Depression

This is where I part company with many of the experts, and I suspect I do so along with many experienced general practitioners. For years the psychiatric establishment analysed and categorized depression into different types according to their different symptoms and severity. We were then given standards by which to classify our patients in practice.

The most common distinction was between 'reactive' and 'endogenous' depression. The differences between these two types of depression seem obvious enough. Reactive depression was thought to be a response to severe stress, something that would naturally make people feel low. It became a depression if it lasted longer, or was more severe, than the normally accepted reaction to a similar stress. Endogenous depression was thought to occur in the absence of any precipitating factor – a depressive illness that somehow arose from inside, that was possibly genetic.

The problem with these definitions is that both types of illness are the same. They don't appear to differ in their character or severity, and to classify them separately doesn't help in their management. Also, if you probe into cases of 'endogenous' depression more deeply, you can usually find some incident that sparked off the current episode of illness. Very few cases arise completely out of the blue. So the distinction between them has been largely abandoned by family doctors like myself.

There are other classifications. One is based on severity – the depression can be mild, moderate or severe. Another concerns whether the illness is purely one of depression or whether it alternates with episodes of mania (the opposite of depression – an unreasonably elated mood). In other words, whether it is 'unipolar' or 'bipolar'. Yet another classification separates neurotic from psychotic depression, in which there may be hallucinations or delusions, or extreme agitation or introversion and slowing of thought and movement.

Classically, neurotic depression is diagnosed when the person persists in dwelling on the experience that sparked off the illness, such as a death in the family or an unexpected loss of a job. The patient is often anxious, but does not have hallucinations (hear, see, smell or feel things that are not there) or delusions (harbour obviously erroneous and usually harm-laden beliefs). They are likely to be quiet and introspective, rather than overactive.

In psychotic depression or manic depressive psychosis, the mood is much more disturbed: people are not only depressed and anxious but may switch often and unexpectedly between these symptoms and bouts of elation and excitement. Along with their delusions they may behave bizarrely, and think and talk so fast that they cannot be understood. They are in particular danger of suddenly and unexpectedly committing suicide. Manic depression recurs at regular intervals, which can sometimes be predicted: it is very important that sufferers are regular attenders at their clinics and take their medication (about which more later).

How useful is this neurotic/psychotic classification? Are they two ends of the same illness, with a gradual merging of the two in the middle in some people? Some evidence that the experts are coming to this view is supported by the fact that many are now abandoning the two terms and just classifying all cases as mild, moderate or severe. That is the new system given by the International Classification of Disease (ICD), the bible by which doctors are now asked to record their diagnoses. I'm not so sure that this is right. One thing is clear. We need two different types of drug to help our patients with neurotic and psychotic depression: this strongly suggests to a family doctor that they are different diseases.

Special Cases
Grief
Defining depression as endogenous/reactive or neurotic/psychotic is largely academic. It is what doctors do when they are putting people into clinical trials of new drugs, and is quite far removed from the everyday practice of treating depression in family practice. Much more useful is to know what to do about particular forms of depression, associated with special circumstances.

The commonest, of course, is the depression that comes with grief. Grief is a natural process that follows the death of a relative, partner or close friend. It has a surprisingly predictable pattern. For the first few days you are numb, and find it difficult to come to terms with the change in your life. The numbness lasts for a few days, usually until after the funeral. The 'pining' phase follows, in which you concentrate on your loss. You have a poor appetite, and you experience lapses in memory and concentration, and become irritable and depressed.

If the grief reaction intensifies after this period, you can despair and become disorganized in your home and at work. You even sense the dead person near you, a feeling that is most acute when you are near to sleep in the evenings. It may take up to a year for the most intense grief to start to settle: if that is your case, you will only begin to get over the worst after the first anniversary of the death, which is naturally always painful.

So grief has three phases. The first is a loss of normal emotional responses: this can last a few days to a few weeks. Second is mourning proper, in which there is yearning for the dead person, somatic symptoms similar to those listed for other forms of depression, and even guilt and denial of death. Third comes acceptance and readjustment to normal life. From phase one to phase three takes around six months for most people. If this process lasts longer, or is blocked by a too-stoic and repressed reaction to the bereavement, or becomes complicated by other signs of psychiatric illness, similar to those described under psychotic depression, then the person needs urgent and continuing treatment. That means counselling (see the chapter on cognitive behaviour therapy), often along with antidepressant drugs. Antidepressants are not given to help people through a normal grief reaction.

Postnatal depression
Giving birth is naturally an emotional time. Hopefully, most of the emotions are uplifting. Most pregnancies are happy affairs, and when they end in a healthy baby and mother (not to mention the father), they are an occasion for rejoicing, not depression.

So when a new mother becomes depressed it can be difficult for those around her to understand. Imagine how much worse it is for the mother herself, who has been looking forward to her baby and all the joys he or she is expected to bring, to find that she is in a deep black hole from which she sees no escape. Add to that the great guilt she feels about being unhappy, her feeling that she does not love her baby as she should, and the total loss of self-esteem that accompanies that feeling, and you start to get the measure of postnatal depression.

It is almost normal to have postnatal 'blues'. Most experts now believe that they are the consequence of the steep fall in female sex hormones, such as progesterone, that occurs as the baby is born. Some women feel the blues are similar to their pre-menstrual tension, just before their periods. If so, they may well share the same cause – progesterone levels fall just before each period appears. We know that there are progesterone receptors on the surface of brain cells: it could well be that the fall in hormone levels directly alters the levels of the brain neurotransmitters mentioned in the last chapter. If so, it could explain the change in mood, and why it comes as an unexpected form of depression with no obvious cause. The next chapter goes into changes in the brain cells in depression more thoroughly.

Postnatal blues start when the baby is less than ten days old, and usually last only a day or two. The mother feels sad, often cries for no apparent reason, then recovers quite quickly. The blues are not a sign of impending postnatal depression: the two are not linked. True postnatal depression may start at any time up to three to four months after the birth. With it come all the symptoms described with depression in the previous few pages. It is no different in type and range of severity from the depression suffered by other adults. However, it does have one further and massive complication: the depressed patient has all the responsibilities that lie in having a new baby to look after. That can put a huge strain on her and her relationships with her partner and the rest of her immediate family and close friends. They must all be extremely supportive and be very careful not to apportion blame or guilt on the hapless mother.

Happily, postnatal depression usually responds well to treatment and is short lived. There is a one-in-seven chance of its returning after the next pregnancy, so it is best for her to be well prepared the next time.

Seasonal Affective Disorder (SAD)
SAD receives a lot of publicity every winter, usually around the New Year. That's the time when newspaper editors are scratching around for a seasonal topic, having exhausted the Christmastime stress, the New Year resolutions and the annual flu epidemic. SAD makes a lot of column inches, too, in the women's magazines, often alongside advertisements for complementary and alternative medicines as winter 'pick me ups'.

The odd thing about SAD is that although there is so much publicity about it, surgery attendances for depression don't seem to vary much throughout the year. In fact, they drop away around Christmas and New Year, as families get together and the seasonal spirit cheers people up. So many family doctors are less convinced than the rest of the public that SAD makes a big contribution to the numbers of people with depression. The World Health Organization (WHO) has yet to define it. However, the Americans have issued their guidelines on how to make the diagnosis of SAD. For what it is worth, here it is:

SAD should be diagnosed if the patient has had at least three periods of depression in three different winter seasons of which at least two should be consecutive. These depressive illnesses (or bipolar illnesses) should occur within the same 60-day winter period in each year. The patient's winter depressions should be three or more times more common than his or her depressions occurring at other times in the year.

It is difficult to substantiate this pattern of depression in any patient. In my rural practice in the West of Scotland, in which daylight lasted only seven hours in mid-winter and it was hardly dark at all in high summer, the peak monthly number of prescriptions for depression was almost always in May. In May there are an average of 15 daylight hours in the 24. Over the five years in which I was the only doctor in the practice, the peak antidepressant prescription rate was never in the months of December to February.

Of course, this is anecdotal evidence from one practice and is not enough on which to base judgement on whether SAD is a separate form of depression from the others. However, it is a pointer that at least in our area of Scotland it is not a significant illness. I would still agree that if people have truly seasonal depression, that hits in the wintertime and eases off in the summer, they should be offered light therapy along with all the standard treatments for depression.

Alcohol
In describing the forms of depression I can't leave out alcohol. I've mentioned earlier that a classic way in which patients with hidden depression present themselves to their doctors is with alcohol abuse. If you are depressed it is tempting to turn to alcohol to 'drown your sorrows'. The phrase is much used, and with good reason, in normal conversation. But there is another side to alcohol and depression. Even if you started drinking just because you like the 'buzz' it gives you, and not because you were depressed, it will leave you with a lowered mood.

Alcohol is not a 'pick me up'. Far from it. It is much more a 'let me down'. Alcohol abuse not only worsens an already depressive illness, it can even initiate it. For a short while alcohol may lighten your mood and loosen your inhibitions, but within as short a time as an hour, that passes. Then you can have many hours of misery as the hangover sets in. If you drink regularly, you are always slightly hung over. This is not just a social thing: alcohol is a powerful drug that slows the brain and directly lowers the mood. All alcoholics are unhappy, no matter how cheerful they seem to be on the surface. If you have a tendency towards depression, the wise answer is to control your drinking. A glass of wine with a meal is fine. Several glasses of any alcoholic drink each day are not.

Other Causes of Depression
So far I have described cases of depression in which it is the main illness. Obviously, many people become depressed because they have good reason to feel low. They may have a long-term illness, like cancer or debilitating arthritis or heart or lung disease. One fairly common cause of depression, physical and mental, is an underactive thyroid. Some psychiatric illnesses, such as schizophrenia, obsessive-compulsive disorders (often referred to in the press as OCD), post-traumatic stress and phobias are linked to depression. In all of these conditions, the aim is to treat the primary illness. As that is eased, the depression usually lifts. However, the treatment for depression in people with any of these illnesses is similar to the treatment of depression per se, which is described later in this book, so I will not dwell on them further.

So, having gone through what depression is, and the many forms it takes, the next question is why people get it. Researchers and those who spend their lives helping people who are depressed have debated this for many years, and still hold to two main schools of thought on the causes of depression. Although they seem far apart, indeed in direct opposition, there is probably truth in both of them. The next chapter explains what we know about the causes of depression now. Recent research into the brain makes it quite different from a similar chapter written, say, in 1990. I'm sure that if I'm re-writing it in 2010, it will be different again.

Chapter Two

Why We Get Depressed – The Two Theories

Do we get depressed because of the circumstances we find ourselves in, or are we born to feel depressed? Or is there an element of both? This is the argument that split psychiatry into two deep divisions for the whole of the last century. In my medical school, the bias was overwhelmingly in favour of the inherited nature of depression. The possibility that we could be born with a normal brain and that we could then be turned into a 'depressive' (our teacher's word) by our surroundings or our circumstances was rejected as nonsense. To emphasize the point, all the Birmingham students were told to buy for our textbook *Clinical Psychiatry* by Professors Willi Mayer-Gross of Birmingham, Dumfries and Heidelberg (he apparently divided his time amongst them), Eliot Slater of London's Institute of Psychiatry and Martin Roth of Newcastle University.

None of these great men had any time for psychoanalysis or for emotional causes for any form of mental illness or mood disturbance. Not for them the inquiry into childhood traumas or stresses at work. They wished psychiatry to be practised and researched under strict scientific rules – and for them that meant that all forms of psychiatric illness must have an underlying biochemical basis, just as does diabetes or arthritis or high blood pressure. The problem for them was that at the time they were writing their august textbook, no one knew anything about the chemistry of the brain.

Today's students might feel that Mayer-Gross, Slater and Roth have been vindicated. Now we do know a lot about brain chemistry. We have discovered dozens of 'neurotransmitters' that convey messages between brain cells in different parts of the brain. Not only that, we know in which parts of the brain each neurotransmitter is most active, or most concentrated, and we know which parts of the brain are associated with different emotional states or moods. And from that we have developed ways of changing neurotransmitter levels and activities within the brain, using drugs especially designed to do so. The whole basis of antidepressant drug theory and practice depends on this knowledge.

So, in theory, we could design a drug that will alter a particular mood in a particular direction, and not cause any other effects. In practice, we have a long way to go to achieve that aim. The drugs we have today are far more effective and specific than the drugs of a few years ago, but they still can't hit the desired target without hitting other, unwanted ones. Hence the fact that so far, any drug that is active against depression or that alters mood has unwanted, as well as the desired, effects.

While we were learning in Birmingham about the biochemical origins of depression, a completely new branch of psychiatric treatment was emerging in other universities. The 'founding father' of this type of treatment was an American psychiatrist, Aaron Beck. While Mayer-Gross and his colleagues were spreading the idea that depression comes first, and gloomy thoughts arise from it, Beck and his followers claimed that negative thoughts came first and led to the depression. The negative thoughts he called 'depressive cognitions', and his way of fighting them was to try to alter the way people thought, so that they would not be so negative. This was christened 'cognitive behaviour therapy'.

In Britain, probably the best-known exponent (to doctors in general practice like myself) of cognitive behaviour therapy is Professor Chris Williams, now of the University of Glasgow, but who worked for many years at the University of Leeds. His book *Overcoming Depression: A Five Areas Approach*, published in Britain by Arnold in 2001, is the best and most useful self-help book on depression for patients and general practitioners. It takes readers with depression through practical ways of changing their thinking and their behaviour, and of reversing the physical symptoms that go with their illness. If you are depressed, I strongly recommend that you buy Chris Williams' book and work your way through each section in turn. However, don't do it on your own. Let your doctor know what you wish to do, and make the self-help system a joint effort. Then, when you come up against problems, you can rely on the family practice team to help you solve them.

So now the battle against depression is being fought on two fronts. The pharmacological front, by which we give drugs to change the biochemistry of the brain, and the 'behaviour' front, by which we aim to change the person's way of thinking and behaving, to avoid and reverse depression.

To which of these groups do I belong? That's a difficult one. By my training and my subsequent career in medical research I tend to favour still the biochemical approach. However, in my practice of family medicine I have been impressed by the results of cognitive behaviour therapy when it is performed with enthusiasm and as part of a team effort. I therefore have a foot in both camps, and as the years pass, the balance seems to be equally on each foot. I'm not falling away in either direction. That's why the treatment section of this book takes in both avenues of treatment and gives them similar emphasis.

Taking the pharmacological side first, the next chapter explains what we know about the brain and how its chemistry can affect our mood. It leads on to the ways in which the chemistry can be altered by drugs acting on the brain. The following chapters describe cognitive behaviour therapy. I stress here that, despite the theories behind their use being so different, and even contradictory, most people with depression can benefit from combining both treatments.

Λ

Chapter Three

Why We Get Depressed – The Role of Brain Biochemistry

What is the evidence that the brain is different in people with depression? There are clues in the family trees of people with depression. Depression does 'run' in families. Studies of close relatives of people with and without depression show clearly that if you have a depressive illness, your family tree will show more first-degree relatives (parent, brother or sister) with depression than the family trees of people without depression. Yet your non-depressed in-law relatives (spouses or spouses of siblings) will not be at a higher risk than normal of depression. Identical twins of someone with depression have a higher risk than non-identical twins or siblings from other pregnancies.

However, the risk varies according to the type of depression. Researchers into the 'nature versus nurture' approach to the origin of depression put the contribution that inheritance makes to manic depression or bipolar disorder (see page 18 for the definitions) at around 80 per cent, and that of the home environment at under 10 per cent. However, in what they define as 'neurotic' depression, the corresponding figures are 10 per cent and over 50 per cent.

I'm not sure how they arrived at these figures, or how accurate they are, but they do suggest an innate contribution to depressive illness from the make-up of the brain. Exactly what that contribution is has taken a lot of very complex research to unravel. At its simplest, it seems that we inherit a tendency to depression that is stimulated when unhappy or unfortunate circumstances come together to bring it to the surface. This process may even occur when there is no preceding circumstance to explain it, which is where the biochemists enter the scene. They propose that such depressions are caused by a change in the neurotransmitters passing between brain cells. Their obvious line of treatment is to try to correct the neurotransmitter imbalance with the correct drugs.

This is also where the cognitive behaviour therapists come in. They would say that people who fall into a depression are 'programmed' to react to such unfortunate circumstances with unhelpful thoughts, faulty behaviour, changed physical feelings and symptoms, and altered emotions. Learning to change all these reactions, they propose, will help people to prevent bouts of depression and to shorten those that do occur. The cognitive behaviour specialists, however, also admit that antidepressant drugs help people to change their inappropriate responses.

So both groups of psychiatrists are in general agreement that the faults lie initially with the brain. Exactly what these faults are has become clearer in the last few years.

Here is where I come to my next recommended reading. It's more difficult reading than Chris Williams' book on *Overcoming Depression* mentioned above, because it is meant for people with a basic knowledge of human biochemistry and cell structures. However, it is ingeniously laid out, with diagrams throughout the book with exceptionally well-explained captions underneath. The title – *Essential Psychopharmacology of Depression and Bipolar Disorder* (Cambridge University Press, 2000) – could put any non-medical reader off, but don't let it do so.

Written by Professor Stephen M Stahl, of the University of California, San Diego, it is meant to be read in two ways. Novices in psychiatry and biochemistry are asked to look only at the colour graphics and their captions, taking them one by one through the book. They should not read the body text of the book until they have gone though all the graphs and diagrams. The first ones illustrate with line graphs the usual progression of the various forms of depressive illness. The middle chapters describe the brain and the areas and pathways within it that are relevant to mood, emotion, reasoning, physical feelings and control. The last chapters show how these change in depression and how drugs that treat depression affect these areas and pathways – and other areas on which we perhaps do not want them to act.

Professor Stahl's diagrams are beautiful and reasonably easy to understand if you read them in sequence. If you have some scientific background and are willing to spend some time learning more about the brain in depression and how your drug treatment changes it, then at least have a look at this book. All the modern drugs, plus most of the old ones, are included in the diagrams, and are explained extremely clearly. Understanding what your drug can do for you, and how long it may take to work fully, can help you through the first, crucial few weeks of your treatment and can give you confidence that you are on the right track, even when you are still feeling awful.

If you are then interested enough to go further, and have a fair knowledge of biological systems, then read the text, too. However, to do that you need to take your time over the first few chapters. It isn't the sort of esoteric and mathematical science that makes Stephen Hawkins' *A Brief History of Time* so difficult to understand, but it does need concentration if you have little or no scientific educational background.

However, I well understand that Professor Stahl's book is beyond what most people need or wish to know about the 'mechanics' of their depression. If you are among them, then please read on here. In the next few pages I will explain as simply as I can what we know about the brain in health and in people with depression. My words are the ones I use when I am explaining depression to patients, one to one, in practice. I hope they make sense to you, because if they don't I'm failing my patients.

The Brain and its Regions and Pathways

To understand the mechanisms that lead to depression, we first have to know something about two aspects of the brain. The first is the way different regions of the brain are responsible for different functions, such as mood, memory, co-ordination, drowsiness/wakefulness, appetite, anxiety, orgasm and ejaculation, nausea and vomiting, and bowel activity (diarrhoea/constipation). We know where each of these aspects of normal living are based in the brain, the types of cells that are in each of these areas, and even the types of neurotransmitter that they produce and pass on to their neighbouring cells.

Diagrams 1 and 2 show where these different centres of control lie in the brain, and their neurotransmitter types. They look complicated, but if you follow the text you will find that they are reasonably easy to understand.

The second aspect of the brain is how each cell communicates with all the others around it. This is where knowledge of the different neurotransmitters and how their activities can be influenced by drugs is vital.

As you read on you may well wonder how we know so much about the workings of the human brain. The early knowledge came from studies of abnormal and normal brain cells taken from people during surgery, say for epilepsy or tumours or after accidents in which some of the damaged brain had to be removed. It is inevitable that during any of these operations the surgeon has to remove not only the diseased or damaged area, but also some of the normal tissues around it. People undergoing such surgery would give their consent for what had to be removed to be kept for research purposes. During the few hours in which such cells could be kept alive, they could be examined for the chemicals they produced.

Now, however, studying pieces of brain removed at operation is only a small part of the research. Researchers can use special scans involving nuclear magnetic resonance (NMR), positron emission tomography (PET) and single photon emission computed tomography (SPECT) to follow the activity of different areas of the brain under circumstances that help define their biochemical activity. They no longer have to dissect a brain or to culture living brain cells to identify what kind of neurotransmitters are active in which circumstances in which area of brain.

There is no need here to explain in detail the methods by which the secrets of the brain have been, and are still being, unravelled: it is enough to state here that it is already established beyond doubt where in the brain the centres for different emotions lie, the type of neurotransmitter that dominates in each of these centres, and the pathways by which these transmitters and centres interconnect.

The figures that follow in these pages show the brain in a person looking to the left. That is, the front of the brain is on the left side, and the back on the right. The names may be complex: they were given to the areas of the brain by anatomists in the nineteenth century, long before they knew what each one did. Those old anatomists were very accurate in their scrutiny of the brain, and they used the international medical language of their time, Latin, in the names they chose. So, for example, *locus caeruleus* simply means 'blue place', which turned out to be quite appropriate for an area that controls depression. Presumably the first anatomists saw a blue tint in that area of the brain in the preserved specimens on which they were working, hence their choice of name. Cortex means 'bark' – as in the bark of a tree, not a dog – and was so named because it was the outer covering of the brain – the grey matter on the surface.

Inside the brain are many nerve 'centres' from which radiate pathways of cell fibres to different areas of the cortex. These centres differ from each other in the neurotransmitters they use as their 'messengers' – the chemicals that are secreted from the end of a cell into the space between it and the next cell. This second cell then picks up the 'message' – the neurotransmitter – which then causes it to spring into activity. That activity is different depending on where the cell is in the cortex. If it is on the side of the brain – the lateral cortex – it might control the contraction of a muscle, so it sends its 'message', using another transmitter along its length, perhaps down the spine, to connect with another nerve that actually causes the muscle to contract.

That's easy to understand. It is the way the brain tells us to walk or to lie down, or to perform any muscular task. Interrupt the messenger pathway, say by damaging your spine, and you are paralysed. No matter how much the cell in your cortex tries to send the message to the muscle, it can't pass through the area of injury.

Take another example. You touch something hot. Nerve endings specially adapted to detect heat react by sending a message up a nerve fibre to a 'junction' near the spine, where a chemical messenger, a neurotransmitter, passes the message to another nerve. By a series of relays of nerve cells, the message eventually reaches the brain, where it is relayed further to the 'sensory' cortex. That's just in front of the 'motor' cortex where the cells controlling the muscles are.

When the neurotransmitter message reaches the sensory cortical cell, it produces the conscious sensation that the fingers have touched a hot surface. Even before you consciously start to pull the fingers away, the message has already been transferred to the appropriate area in the motor cortex, via yet another neurotransmitter, to start the action of removing the fingers from the heat.

You may think that feeling pain and drawing your fingers away from it are a 'natural' part of your life, and may never before have considered that the process happens quite outside your conscious control – but it does. Think again about what happens when you come up against a painful stimulus – you draw away from it at the moment you register the pain, and before you have made the conscious decision to do so.

Every second of your life your brain is controlling actions of which you are completely unconscious. Such as how wide open the pupils of your eyes are, or how fast your heart is beating and with what force. Or how fast your gut is moving your food from stomach to anus. Or how you balance yourself when walking.

It is only when something happens to your brain to cause you to lose this unconscious control of your activities that you begin to appreciate how vital they are to you. The most obvious example to most people is after a stroke, when they lose the ability to walk because half the body has been paralysed. But there are many more subtle examples, not so well known, that begin to explain change in mood.

For example, if the stroke affects certain parts of the front of the brain, it may cause the person to become more aggressive than before, so that his or her character seems to change. Brain tumours or injuries, say after accidents, affecting different parts of the brain can cause people to be depressed or inappropriately elated, or even react to circumstances in ways that are completely out of character. Crying rather than laughing at humour, or laughing when told of a death are extreme cases of this.

Parkinson's disease affects one particular part of the brain, the basal ganglia. Degeneration of a very small area of basal ganglia cells leads to people having great difficulty with movement. They become very stiff, find it very difficult to move muscles smoothly and quickly, and when they are resting they shake constantly. These reactions are all the result of problems with the production and activity of a neurotransmitter, called DOPA.

In Alzheimer's, the brain damage not only leads to loss of memory and intellect, but to a general slowing of all thought, and with that also often comes a degree of depression, even when the person has no insight into his or her illness. In other words, the depression is not a conscious (and wholly understandable) reaction to the illness, but an innate result of problems of communications between the damaged brain cells.

To understand what happens in depression, all that is needed is to make the leap from accepting the evidence that neurotransmitters are involved in brain damage in these different illnesses to accepting the evidence that they are involved in producing depression. Think back to that motor cell whose neurotransmitter action made the muscles contract, then think of the cell in a different part of the cortex that is responsible for mood. When it is stimulated, instead of making a muscle work, or making you become conscious of pain, it lightens your mood. And if it is not working properly, perhaps not being sensitive enough to its neurotransmitter, then you feel blue instead.

To feel blue, therefore, all you need is a disturbed neurotransmitter system. The converse of that is that to feel better, you need to put the neurotransmitter system back on the right wavelength. That is the basis of all drug treatment for depression.

So what are these neurotransmitters, and how do they influence our mood in health and disease? For the moment, we know of three that are definitely implicated in depression: they are called noradrenaline (norepinephrine in North America), serotonin (sometimes called 5-hydroxytryptamine or 5-HT) and dopamine. There are probably others, but these three have been the subject of the bulk of the research.

Each of these 'sets' of nerves with different types of transmitter has a different 'centre' deep in the brain, which contains the nerve 'cell bodies'. Nerve cells have three essential components. They have dendrites, fibre-like extensions that 'pick up' the message from the previous cell in the chain. The dendrites pass the message inside the cell to the cell body. In the cell body, the nucleus (the 'brain' of the cell) and mitochondria (the 'factory' inside the cell) process the information they receive, respond to it, and pass on their response to the third part of the cell, the axon. Cells have many dendrites, but only one axon. The axon is the fibre-like extension of the cell that carries the message from the cell body to the site where it has to pass on its message to the next part of the brain – to the dendrites of the next nerve cell in the chain. The diagram (See overleaf) shows how they work together.

Noradrenaline
The centre for the noradrenaline transmitter system (that is, the site of all the cell bodies that have axons that secrete noradrenaline) is in the *locus caeruleus*. This is deep in the 'brain stem', where the top of the spinal cord meets the lower surface of the brain. The axons from the nerves in the *locus caeruleus* fan out in the pathways shown in the

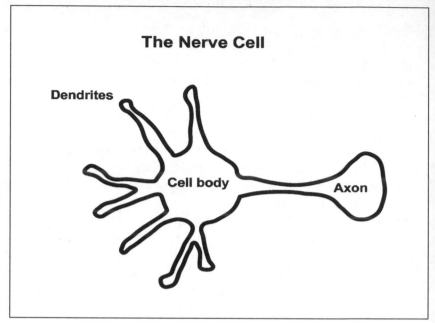

The Nerve Cell

Dendrites

Cell body

Axon

Figure 1: Diagram of a Nerve Cell

next diagram – to the front and sides of the cortex and into the cerebellum in the back of the brain. Axons that secrete noradrenaline from their ends are called noradrenergic nerves, and the system of nerves that do so, collectively, is called the adrenergic system.

The noradrenergic pathways to the front of the brain (the frontal cortex) are thought to be responsible for lightening mood. To the cortex just to one side of this are the pathways for attention, concentration and cognition (memory, reasoning, understanding and speed of thought). The noradrenergic nerves to the part of the brain just underneath the frontal cortex, called the limbic area stimulate emotions and control the balance between energy and fatigue. They also determine whether you are agitated or calm and how quickly or slowly you think and move. The adrenergic pathways to the cerebellum (at the back of the brain) control the smoothness of muscle contraction. When it goes wrong the limbs tremble – or are in a state of 'tremor'. Pathways back from the *locus caeruleus* down into the brain stem control blood pressure, and other pathways leading down the spinal cord and into the chest

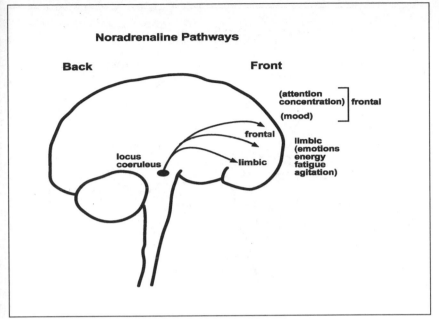

Figure 2: Diagram of the Noradrenaline Nerve Network
(Adapted from page 30 of Professor Stahl's book.)

chest control the heart rate. Finally, adrenergic nerves from the *locus caeruleus* pass further down the spine to reach the bladder, where they control feelings of bladder fullness, the desire to urinate and the act of urination itself.

You may now be realizing that when your noradrenergic system starts to go wrong, depression may be only part of a host of symptoms that you will surely recognize. Along with the depression, your ability to concentrate may fail, your memory isn't what it was and your muscle co-ordination isn't as good. You may be anxious, or shake, or feel constantly tired and not be as sharp mentally as you were. You may even have problems with low or high blood pressure, a fast or slowed heartbeat and an irritable bladder that makes you keep running, often fruitlessly, to the toilet.

The corollary to this is that, if you are given a drug to try to correct your depression by acting on your noradrenergic nerves, some of these symptoms may actually become worse, rather than better.

This is why so many antidepressant drugs have a long list of side effects on their pack leaflets. In fact, they are not truly side effects, but

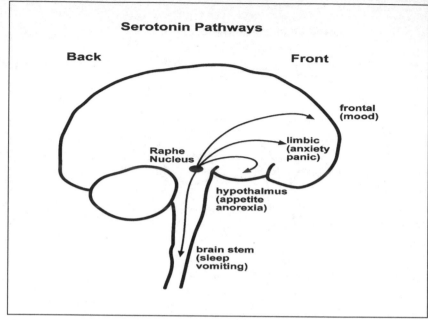

Figure 3: Diagram of the Serotonin Nerve Pathways
(From pages 48–50 of Professor Stahl's book.)

the main effects of the drugs. Much depends on the areas on which each drug works and what action it has upon them. The host of modern drugs prescribed for depression includes many with different actions, so that if you suffer side effects with one type of antidepressant, another one may not produce them.

Serotonin

The control area for the serotonin-producing nerves (serotonergic nerves) is in the raphe nucleus, in the brain stem, close to the *locus caeruleus* (see Figure 1). Like the noradrenergic system, axons radiate out from the raphe to other parts of the brain, and they release serotonin from their endings. Those that do so in the frontal cortex, like the noradrenergic nerves there, regulate your mood. Those passing to the basal ganglia in the middle of the brain help us to control our movements, and also control our tendencies to obsessive and compulsive behaviour. Agitation and repetitive movements may be controlled by serotonergic nerves in this area.

Serotonergic nerves going from the raphe to the limbic area, on the lower surface of the cortex, are active in states of anxiety and panic, and probably phobias. Similar nerves passing to the hypothalamus, under the base of the brain and just above the pituitary gland, control appetite and eating behaviour, such as bingeing and starving.

Other serotonergic nerves pass down into the brain stem, just where it merges into the spinal cord, to control sleep. Further down the spinal cord, serotonergic nerves control sexual excitation, including erection in men, vaginal and clitoral sensation in women, and orgasm in both sexes. Serotonergic nerves deep in the brain stem control the sensation of nausea and the muscular contractions of vomiting.

Dopamine
Dopaminergic nerves (which secrete dopamine from the ends of their axons) are found throughout the brain. They function alongside noradrenergic and serotonergic nerves within the brain, sometimes acting to potentiate their activities, sometimes to control and even reverse them. Drugs that work on dopaminergic nerves have mainly found their uses in Parkinson's disease and schizophrenia. The use of them in such illnesses is outside the scope of this book. However, some newer antidepressant drugs combine noradrenergic, serotonergic and dopaminergic actions, so dopamine is mentioned here for completeness.

When the Neurones go Wrong
So exactly what happens when these systems go wrong? How do we become depressed? This is where the study of the brain becomes less than an exact science. With our present state of knowledge we can only make informed guesses, but the guesswork is receding year by year as the researchers learn more. What seems to happen is described below.

Fundamental to the health of a cell is the number and activity of the dendrites. The more dendrites a cell has, the more connections it can make (through picking up neurotransmitter 'messages') with its neighbouring cells. The more connections the cell has, and the faster it can deal with them, the more active it is. The fewer the dendrites, the less active it is, and the less able it is to pick up messages from the neurotransmitters secreted by its neighbours. A good example of what happens when this system fails is in

Alzheimer's disease, where dendrites are lost or become entangled so that they cannot pass on messages. The cells then can't intercommunicate, and loss of memory and intellect follows.

Cells 'grow' dendrites under the influence of a substance called brain-derived neurotrophic factor, or BDNF. (The language seems complex, but it really isn't. Neuro stands for nerve, and trophy is the biological word for growth. So a neurotrophic factor causes nerve cells to grow, and this particular factor is found in the brain, hence brain-derived.)

In the non-depressed brain, the gene for making BDNF is normal, BDNF is produced in normal amounts, and cells have a large number of dendrites, which gather information and pass it on. It is suggested that in people with an inherited tendency to depression, the BDNF gene is faulty. It cannot make the extra amount it needs to under conditions of stress. So instead of stress causing the neurones to grow and cope by producing extra dendrites, they change in the other direction. They lose dendrites, they carry fewer messages, and they may even atrophy and die. The concentrations of neurotransmitters between the neurones fall, and depression is the result.

With repeated episodes of depression, there are fewer and fewer dendrites, and the bouts of depression become more severe, longer, and more resistant to treatment. Scans of the brain in people with long-term severe depression, or who are in the throes of an acute bout of depression, suggest that the neurones in the brain centres to do with depression are either smaller in size or they are functioning much less efficiently than normal.

What can we do with this knowledge? The short answer is to design drugs that will reverse these changes – to stimulate the correct nerve cells and to increase their activity, and to improve the amount of neurotransmitter to which they are exposed. That has been the whole thrust of research into antidepressant drugs over the last 40 years. There have been some great successes, but none are perfect. The next chapter summarizes those that are used in practice today, what they do to the brain, their effects on depression and their side effects.

Chapter Four

Treating Depression with Drugs

Most people with depression are not ill all the time. Depression is an illness of cycles. If you have depression, you will probably recognize that it comes and goes. It's common for people to be depressed for between six months and two years at a time, then to feel better, sometimes for many years, before another episode turns up, as if out of the blue. People who have had several depressive illnesses can almost predict, from their past experience, when they will have the next one.

In fact, that's another piece of the jigsaw of evidence that depression is an innate illness affecting the brain chemistry and not a reaction to circumstances. Their cycle of depression does not follow a pattern of cycles of life stresses.

So the aim of treatment is to try to shorten your period of depression, and then to prevent the next one from appearing. That means, usually, that once you start on an antidepressant drug, if it works and the side effects are tolerable, you should stay on it for a year or two before thinking of stopping it.

The aim of treatment, of course, is cure. That is to make you feel well, and to keep you feeling well for the foreseeable future. It isn't always easy with drugs alone, or for that matter with cognitive behaviour therapy alone (see the following chapters for its explanation). It is estimated by most researchers that only around two-thirds of people who take antidepressant drugs feel much better on them, and maintain that feeling for more than six months. That is better than the one-third who improve on placebo (dummy tablets made to look like the real thing). They were probably in the recovery phase of their current depressive episode at the time of the drug trial.

However, we do not have to stick to one drug or type of drug in our efforts to achieve a cure. The first truly active drugs on disturbed mental states were the 'phenothiazines', developed more than 50 years ago from similar drugs given initially to cure tuberculosis.

Doctors noticed that patients who had both psychiatric illnesses and tuberculosis who were given a phenothiazine for tuberculosis not only became physically better, but also became less mentally ill. They were first used in schizophrenia, and it was only a few steps on from there to develop drugs, now called tricyclics from their chemical structure (the molecule contained three 'carbon rings'), that might work in depression.

Tricyclics

We still have a class of drugs called the tricyclics today. If you have depressive illnesses, you may well have taken them at some time – and even now may be on them. They include, in alphabetic order of their 'generic' name:

- amitriptyline (Tryptafen)
- amoxapine (Asendis)
- clomipramine (Anafranil)
- doxepin (Sinequan)
- imipramine (Tofranil)
- maprotiline (Ludiomil)
- nortriptyline (Allegron, Motival)
- trimipramine (Surmontil).

It must be remembered that when the tricyclics were first introduced, they were a huge step forward in our ability to treat depression. Not only did they work, but they kept on working, and unlike drugs like tranquillizers, which were introduced at around the same time for anxiety, they were not addictive. Nor did their beneficial effects wear off.

But they did, and still do, cause side effects. The diagrams of the neurotransmitter pathways in the previous chapter explain why they do. In effect they are five drugs in one. They have effects on noradrenaline and serotonin that are beneficial for depression, but they have other, less desired, effects on acetylcholine (which alters our ability to focus, our production of saliva, and the activities of our gut, bladder and heart). They also have antihistamine and sedative properties (so they increase appetite and make us drowsy), and they can block receptors that control our blood pressure (so they can lower the blood pressure).

Tricyclics can therefore be very effective in treating depression, but can leave you overweight, constantly sleepy, with constipation, bladder problems, blurred vision and a dry mouth. You may also have dizzy spells, particularly when rising from a sitting or lying position, because their effect on blood pressure control limits the blood flow to the head when you stand up.

So if you are taking a tricyclic you have to weigh up the benefits against your experience of the disadvantages. Some people find the side effects trivial and easily borne, whilst others find them disabling and need to stop the treatment. Many people manage to tolerate the side effects for a while, perhaps even a few months, because they feel the benefit of their brighter mood. However, the prospect of having to cope with them for years at a time eventually becomes too much, and they stop their drugs early. If they do that without consulting their doctor, they run a high risk of their depression returning.

Selective Serotonin Reuptake Inhibitors (SSRIs)

SSRIs sound complicated, but don't let the four initials put you off trying to understand what they do. In fact, the process is quite simple. Brain cells not only push out serotonin into the space between them and their neighbours, they also have a 'pump' system that takes it up again. So a drug that blocks the 're-uptake' pump leaves more serotonin in the space between the cells. That keeps the level of the serotonin 'message' higher between the cells.

Another look at the diagrams of the neurotransmitter pathways shows which areas this action is likely to stimulate, such as:

- the frontal cortex (in the front of the brain), to lift mood
- the basal ganglia, to reduce obsessions and compulsions
- the limbic area, to ease anxiety and panic
- the hypothalamus, to normalize appetite and eating disorders
- the brain stem, to regulate sleep
- the spinal cord, to help sexual responses, such as orgasm and ejaculation
- the brain stem, to control nausea

There are also serotonin receptors in the gut wall, which co-ordinate normal bowel movement.

You might think from this list that SSRIs are a panacea for all emotional and mood disturbances, but unfortunately they are not. Human biology is not an exact science, so that a rising serotonin level between brain cells suits some people and not others. Changing your brain serotonin levels may lighten the mood of a lot of people, but in others it may unleash aggressive behaviour and even violent thoughts.

A BBC *Panorama* television programme highlighted what appeared to be serious side effects of the drug Seroxat (paroxetine). Several people spoke about their experience of violent nightmares, and some had even been violent towards their family in the first few days of starting the drug.

It is always dangerous to draw firm conclusions about a drug from a few case histories. The only way to make sure that a drug is safe, as well as effective, is to look at the statistics of many people who have been in trials comparing it with other drugs or placebo (a similar looking and tasting tablet or capsule in which there is no active ingredient). The initial large-scale trials of Seroxat failed to show such an effect. However, it would seem wise for anyone who experiences a bad change in mood in the first few days after starting a course of Seroxat or any other SSRI to report it immediately to his or her doctor. The usual course would then be to substitute another antidepressant of a different kind in its place.

It is important to understand that with any drug which acts directly on brain neurotransmitters there will be some side effects in some people that may be unpleasant. It may be that increasing the serotonin levels in their brains may trigger some unwanted (and unusual, from the small numbers of people affected by it) response. If this is your own experience, then that type of drug is not for you. However, there are others that you may try; they are described in the next few pages. It has to be said here that the vast majority of people put on SSRIs by doctors or consultant psychiatrists are improved by them, and are happy to be taking them.

SSRIs available in Britain at the time of writing (summer 2003) include:

- citalopram (Cipramil)
- escitalopram (Cipralex)
- fluoxetine (Prozac)
- fluvoxamine (Faverin)
- paroxetine (Seroxat)
- sertraline (Lustral).

According to the textbooks, SSRIs are better tolerated than tricyclics. They are said to make people less sleepy, to have less effect on the bowel and bladder, to be safer for the heart and to be less likely to cause death if an overdose is taken. So it was expected that by now they would have replaced the older tricyclics as the treatment of choice for most cases of depression.

This is happening, but quite slowly. In the *British Medical Journal* of 10 May 2003, Dr Steve McGillivray and his colleagues at the University of Dundee analysed 11 studies comparing tricyclics with SSRIs. They showed that the two types of drug were equally effective in lifting depression, and that many more patients receiving a tricyclic than receiving an SSRI stopped their treatment because of side effects. Patients being treated by their general practitioners were more likely to continue with an SSRI than with a tricyclic. There was less difference in tolerance to the two types when patients were treated by hospital-based psychiatrists.

Some patients who have tried both still prefer the tricyclics to the SSRIs. Presumably many of them are people who suffer from the side effects listed in the drug leaflets that are given with each prescription – they include nausea, diarrhoea, headache, insomnia, agitation and sexual dysfunction (failure to have an orgasm or an ejaculation, less often impotence).

Other Options

Tricyclics and SSRIs are the drugs of first choice for most people with depression, but if you can't tolerate them, or find that they are just not working for you, then there are others. Like the SSRIs, they are identified by their initials.

They include SNRIs, such as venlafaxine (Efexor). They act by blocking the re-uptake of two neurotransmitters, serotonin and noradrenaline – hence the SNRI label. Like the SSRIs, they have many fewer side effects than the tricyclics. Venlafaxine is often used as a first-line treatment today, particularly in older patients who are constantly sad (a state that doctors still call melancholia, the old name for depression), or are anxious, agitated or very slow in their thoughts (a condition psychiatrists call retardation).

Then there are NARIs, such as reboxetine (Edronax). They are selective in blocking the reuptake of noradrenaline only. They, too, have fewer side effects than tricyclics. Whether they are more effective than them is still a matter of debate.

NASSAs (noradrenaline and selective serotonin antidepressants) act in a different way from the reuptake inhibitors. They increase the transmission of noradrenaline and serotonin from the brain cells. The first drug in this class is mirtazapine (Zispin). It is said to avoid the SSRI side effects of nausea, insomnia, anxiety, agitation and sexual dysfunction. However, its official side effect list includes weight gain, drowsiness, liver problems, fluid retention leading to oedema (soft tissue swelling, especially around the ankles), rashes and mania. Very rarely it can cause a fall in white blood cell counts, making people more than usually susceptible to infection. People on mirtazapine are warned to let their doctors know immediately they have an infection or note the first signs of jaundice.

MAOIs need a mention here, too. They are the 'monoamine oxidase' inhibitors. Neurotransmitters such as noradrenaline and serotonin are broken down (their effects neutralized) by substances known as monoamine oxidases (MAOs). Block the action of an MAO, and the transmitter that it breaks down will remain in the tissue, continuing to stimulate the relevant cells.

MAOIs have been used since the 1970s. They include phenelzine (Nardil), tranylcypromine (Parnate) and moclobemide (Manerix). They are very effective in relieving depression, but the first two, the oldest MAOIs, have a severe drawback. This is because they block the breakdown of other monoamines in the body besides the ones that cause depression in the brain. This can have serious, and even fatal, consequences if MAOIs are taken with drugs or foods that give rise to large amounts of monoamines. I need not go into the chemistry of all the monoamines they affect, but the important ones are responsible for regulating the blood pressure and for handling the elimination of substances such as alcohol, sedatives, insulin and narcotic painkillers such as morphine derivatives from the body.

So people taking phenelzine or tranylcypromine must take great care to avoid foods containing high levels of substances that produce monoamines in the body. They include cheese, meat extracts such as Bovril or Oxo, yeast extracts such as Marmite, broad beans, wines, beers or spirits (even low-alcohol drink), pickles and flavoured textured vegetable proteins prepared for vegetarians.

Why should people taking these drugs be so restricted in their eating choices? Taking an MAOI and eating or drinking any of these food items can steeply increase blood pressure, to heights that can cause strokes or sudden heart failure. It is important for people asked to try taking an MAOI to make sure that the doctor prescribing it knows about any other drug they may be taking. MAOIs must not be taken along with other antidepressants, with sleeping tablets, with certain types of painkillers, or with treatments for diabetes such as insulin or tablets to lower blood glucose levels, as they can cause severe reactions in all these cases.

If you are asked to take an MAOI, you must accept the discipline of great care in what you eat and in the other drugs you take, otherwise you are putting yourself at risk. The risk is probably less with the newest MAOI, moclobemide, the effects of which are easier to reverse than those of phenelzine and tranylcypromine.

With so many serious side effects, MAOIs are kept as third- or even fourth-line treatment after other drugs have failed. Switching to them from another antidepressant is not straightforward. For example, you may have to wait several weeks after stopping an SSRI before starting on an MAOI, as it takes a long time to eliminate the last vestiges of the SSRI from your body – and that's important in preventing a severe reaction to the new drug. The gap may be up to five weeks for the switch from fluoxetine – and that can be a long time without medication for someone with depression. The same goes for replacing an MAOI with an SSRI. Doctors are advised to wait two complete weeks after stopping a patient's MAOI before starting him or her on an SSRI.

Other Antidepressants

If you haven't responded well enough to your first treatments, or you haven't been able to tolerate their side effects, and you don't think you are disciplined enough to take MAOIs, there are still others your doctor can try.

The experts lump them together in a category of 'Other antidepressants' largely because the way they work on the brain is still not clear. I have grouped them together here because they are, like MAOIs, used either when other drugs have failed, or because the type of depression the patient suffers from seems to suit that particular drug's action. Here they are in no special order of efficacy:

- *Trazodone (Molipaxin)*: It has an 'anti-serotonin' action in the laboratory, which is presumably not how it works in an actual patient, as this would seem to deepen depression. However, it may stimulate noradrenaline activity in the brain. It is used for depression with anxiety, as it tends to lessen anxiety, and for depression with insomnia, as it helps people to sleep. It has fewer and milder side effects than tricyclics, and is less likely to cause death in an overdose.

- *Maprotiline (Ludiomil)*: Maprotiline's chemical structure makes it a 'tetracyclic', rather than a tricyclic (the molecule has a four-ringed structure rather than three rings). It mainly blocks the reuptake of noradrenaline, and has no effect on serotonin. Its main advantage over tricyclics is that it produces very few heart and gut side effects. It is mainly used for patients for whom tricyclics are effective in improving depression, but are not tolerable because of their side effects.

- *Lithium (Liskonum, Li-Liquid)*: Lithium is used to treat both mania (extreme 'highs') and depression (extreme 'lows') in patients with severe manic depression. We don't know how it works, but it is thought to reduce noradrenaline levels in the brain. Its aim is to keep mood steady in people who suffer from extreme swings in mood that are not only very distressing for them, but also may make them a danger to themselves or others. If you are taking lithium you must have your blood level of lithium measured regularly (usually once a week) to make sure it is in the right range. If it is too low it is unlikely to work: too high and it can cause severe adverse effects, such as trembling, weakness, digestive upsets, weight gain, fluid retention, thirst, rashes, blurred vision, taste disturbances, sexual problems and high blood sugar levels that may even mimic diabetes. So if you are taking lithium, you need to keep in close touch with your medical team.

- *Flupenthixol (Fluanxol)*: This is mainly reserved for people with schizophrenia whose main symptoms include apathy, lowered mood, weakness and despondency.

- *Carbamazepine (Tegretol)*: This was never intended to be an anti-depressant. It has been used for many years in two conditions – to prevent convulsions in epilepsy, and to relieve the pain of trigeminal neuralgia (a severe pain in the face caused by pressure on a nerve as it emerges from the skull). It is only in recent years that it has been found to improve depression in people with manic depression whose moods swing between high and low several times a year. It is an alternative to lithium, with fewer side effects. We are not sure how it works. It acts in epilepsy and in trigeminal neuralgia by decreasing the electrical activity in the nerves that are the focus of the convulsions and the pain. It may do the same in nerve pathways in the brain, overactivity of which can cause depression. Some researchers believe the site may be in a part of the brain called the limbic system, but that still has to be proven.

Summarizing Drugs for Depression

If you have managed to read through this chapter without becoming confused, well done. It is a complicated subject, and enough to make you depressed if you think about it too much. That's bad enough for someone like me, who is fortunate enough not to be depressed and who has had seven years of extra training, over and above what I learned at medical school, on the effects and side effects of drugs. It is even worse for you, if you started off depressed and with no training.

So, to cut through the complexities, here is a short summary on the current (2003) status of drugs treatment for depression.

Around half of all people with depression are still being treated with tricyclics. Each one differs from all the others in its dose, how often it should be given, and how quickly you feel an improvement once you start taking it. They also differ in the rates and severity of their side effects. However, you can't predict how a particular tricyclic will affect you. What suits one person may not suit another.

Often it is a case of trial and error until you and your doctor find the one that helps lift your mood with the fewest and mildest side effects.

Most of the other half of the population with depression are taking one of the many SSRIs. A small minority are taking the 'other' drugs. As with the tricyclics, it may take time to find the one that suits you. Your doctor and your practice nurse will help you through the first few months until you find the best treatment.

Whatever the drug that is chosen for you, it is vital that you understand one thing. You will begin to feel better, hopefully after a week or two (don't expect instant relief). When you do, DON'T think of stopping. Your depression is not cured, it is just being managed. If you stop your course of drugs early, you may well experience a 'rebound' in your symptoms, so that you descend steeply back into a deep depression. Most doctors, once they have started to prescribe an antidepressant for a patient, will insist on at least six months of treatment. My own experience suggests that a two-year course is preferable, and probably the minimum for most patients. It can take that time to help the brain adjust to normal brain transmitter patterns. So don't expect to come off your drugs early.

Never stop the drugs yourself. Always seek your doctor's advice before changing the dose or stopping. People who stop them abruptly can experience serious withdrawal symptoms, such as nightmares and severe swings in mood. You need help and supervision when you eventually stop the course.

Chapter Five

ECT and Other Treatments

Electroconvulsive therapy (ECT) has had a bad press for many years. That's not surprising. Passing powerful electric currents through the brain is a pretty shocking thing to do in both senses of the word. Each session of ECT leaves the patient confused and with gaps in his or her memory, and it takes many hours to recover back to a normal state. Over the years, there have been countless reports from people who have had ECT and from their relatives and friends of the damage that it may do.

Yet ECT is still used, and many experts in depression treatment consider it to have a definite place for patients in whom other antidepressant treatments have failed. I must admit here that I became biased against it, as I mentioned in my foreword, in my student years, when I had to witness long-stay 'mental' patients (as they were described then) having their ECT treatments.

I have changed my mind a little since then because I have had patients in general practice who were deeply depressed, unresponsive to other treatments, who responded especially well to ECT. They do have permanent problems with their memory of the time around which they were in hospital for their depression, but they see that as a minor drawback in comparison with their current feelings of wellbeing. In fact, at least two of them are grateful for their memory loss: they have no wish to remember what they consider as among the worst times of their lives.

In my experience of a small number of patients who eventually had to have ECT, all of them found that it lifted their depression, and for most the better mood lasted a long time. One woman, who had been suicidal in her mid-thirties, dates her new life from her series of ten ECT treatments. Now in her fifties, she has not had a period of depression since. She states that she would have been dead by now if she had not been given the ECT. From my knowledge of the depth of her depression and despair before she had the ECT, and the transformation since, I'm certain she is right.

Even though she had her treatment in the days before SSRIs, I'm not sure they would have had the dramatic depression-relieving effect that the ECT had upon her. They are relatively slow in having a significant effect. Even if she had had them in those days, she might well have carried out her threat to kill herself in days before the drug worked. In this woman, however, the cure has come at a price. She feels 'she may have lost something' since her ECT, and her husband, though delighted now to have a happy wife, says she still has a few memory lapses. Whether this is really a long-term effect of the ECT, or just a coincidence, can't be known.

So how does ECT work? Superficially it seems to be more witchcraft than medicine. Its opponents compare it to the practice of doctors in ancient Greece, of throwing mentally ill people into pits full of snakes: their reasoning was that the fright was so great they would be shocked back into health. It is said that this is part of the explanation of the universal medical symbol that dates back to classical Greece, of the serpents entwined on a staff.

Supporters of ECT explain its use in more modern terms. They see it as causing the brain to have an epileptic convulsion. This is thought to release a host of neurotransmitters from the assaulted brain cells, among them noradrenaline and serotonin. The problem with explaining ECT in this way is that no one has actually measured these substances in the human brain before and after it is used. Until someone does, we can't know what we are doing when we expose the depressed brain to such a shock. I'm not happy about reporting the experiments in animals undergoing ECT, mainly because the human brain is so different from that of other animals, and partly because I wonder about the ethics of putting animals through it if little can be learned from them. But the experiments have been done, and they show that ECT has opposing effects on noradrenaline and serotonin release in the animal brain. Whether such results can be used to make newer antidepressants that will act much faster than current ones in humans remains to be seen.

Whatever its underlying mechanism of action, ECT remains the fastest way to reverse depression, and this can be life-saving in people who are so depressed that they are bent on suicide, or who have not responded at all to other treatments. So it is still used all over the world – in some countries much more often than in others. Much depends on the attitudes of the psychiatrists in individual hospitals, as well as on the guidelines laid down by each individual country's psychiatric authorities.

Most developed countries now use ECT along with an anaesthetic and a muscle relaxant drug, so that the patient does not feel any discomfort and there is no actual convulsion. Having relaxed muscles during the treatment prevents any physical harm and does away with the need for restraint. The modern ECT room is much more patient friendly and much less frightening than the desperate places I had to attend as a raw student. The staff are much more friendly, too. Gone are the matter-of-fact male nurses of two generations ago (in the hospital I worked in there were only male nurses for male patients), to be replaced by the extremely sympathetic, caring and well-trained nursing staff of today.

So the fear has been removed, as far as is humanly possible, from ECT. Yet it still attracts a lot of opposition. That is why most countries have strict rules (they are called guidelines, but they had better be obeyed) about its use. The American Psychiatric Association has proposed that doctors should think of referring patients for ECT only if they:

- care severely depressed
- need very urgent relief of their depression because they may harm themselves
- are not responding to, or have reacted with intolerable side effects to, drug treatments
- care agreeable to undergo ECT, having had its benefits and drawbacks explained to them in full without any pressure being put upon them to accept it

Most British psychiatrists would probably agree with these conditions. However, the debate continues. Some reports suggest that 80 to 90 per cent of seriously depressed people respond well to ECT (reference E Persad, 'Electroconvulsive therapy in depression', *Canadian Journal of Psychiatry*, 1990, volume 35, pages 175-82). Others claim that many of the patients in ECT studies were not truly non-responders to drug treatments (a requisite for most of the trials), but had not had adequate doses of the drugs (reference S L Dubovsky and M Thomas, 'Approaches to the treatment of refractory depression', *Journal of the Practice of Psychiatry and Behaviour*

Health, 1996, volume 2, pages 14-22). They might have done just as well if their drug doses had been higher. I would add that they might have done just as well, too, if they had had more modern drugs. Most of the ECT studies were performed in the 1970s and 1980s, when we did not have the latest antidepressant drugs.

Some psychiatrists have advocated using ECT in people with heart problems, in whom the side effects of antidepressant drugs might be dangerous (reference K Franco-Bronson, 'The management of treatment-resistant depression in the medically ill', *Psychiatric Clinics of North America*, 1996, volume 19, pages 329-50). I'm not sure that this is still an arguable case for ECT, as the newer antidepressant drugs have much less action on the heart than the tricyclics. However, it is reassuring to know that if ECT is needed, having a heart condition is not a drawback to it. Of course, each person needs to be assessed for his or her own risks, and no use of anaesthesia or ECT is without risk in itself.

How many ECTs should the patient have? Hospital practice differs widely: some psychiatrists prefer to give courses of six or more, others fewer. These are given at different intervals, sometimes depending on the patient's response. And, of course, the patient always has the choice of refusing it. Nowadays we don't – as I witnessed years ago – drag unwilling patients into the room and give them treatment against their will. Thank goodness those days of what could only be described as brutality are long over.

Perhaps the best way to end this chapter is to quote from Willi Mayer-Gross's *Clinical Psychiatry*, published in 1960, when ECT was the best antidepressant therapy he could offer (reference W Mayer-Gross, E Slater and M Roth, *Clinical Psychiatry*, Cassell, 1960, pages 224-7). He writes:

The mistake that is most frequently made nowadays is its excessive or too indiscriminate use. The authors have seen no good results from battering the patient with more than one fit a day for days in succession, but they have seen the most serious and lasting losses of memory and amnesic patches extending over months or even years as a result of this treatment, which then themselves form the germ of new complaints.

It is staggering to think that people could be subjected to more than one ECT a day for many days in succession. The practice smacks of sadism. He continues:

It is probably best to give the treatment twice a week for the first three or four treatments, after which it can be given once weekly. If no sign of improvement has been obtained with the first six treatments it is best to revert to more conservative measures for one or two months, after which a second attempt can be made.

This advice on treatments is probably much the same as would be given today, except that few people will be offered a second course if a first course has failed.

But I don't want to end this chapter on a negative note. Professor Mayer-Gross loved his anecdotes, and he has a beauty to illustrate the benefits of ECT. He quotes from a patient's letter to him, written three years after her discharge from hospital:

After the second treatment I could taste my food for the first time and felt that I had an appetite. I had been so fond of sweets and after I got depressed I could not look at them. Just after the second treatment one of the ladies gave me a bit of chocolate. It tasted so good and I just wanted more, and I got better every day after that. I could not bear to hear a bird singing or hear the sound of a motor horn when I went in at first. After the electrical treatment everything was different. I certainly have felt no bad effects and I can concentrate on reading, sewing, wireless or listening even to a quarrel with my two girls and I never bother at all.

If you are depressed you will certainly recognize his description of this lady's desperate state of mind, and the joy she had in recovery from it. If ECT is the only way to achieve such a recovery, it is surely worthwhile. The problem comes when it doesn't work. I wonder how many letters Professor Mayer-Gross received from patients who had bad experiences with ECT?

Remember that his patients were being treated before people were given general anaesthetics (they were simply sedated, but still half conscious when they received their shock). So he writes: 'It seems unnecessary to start with the lowest possible dose in each case because subconvulsive shocks (i.e. electric shocks that you feel because you are still conscious) are often very unpleasant for the patient and apt to increase his apprehension.' I bet they did!

Naturally, it was scenes like this that gave ECT so much bad publicity, and rightly so. Today it is so different. If you are being advised to have ECT, do talk it over with your psychiatrist, your doctor and the staff who work in the unit. They will give you a complete explanation of what will happen, and be very reassuring and sympathetic. The bad days are gone. And remember that you have the final word. If you don't want it, just say no. Everyone will understand and be happy with your decision. You will not be letting anyone down, including yourself, if you don't want to go through with it.

A recent review of ECT in England was published in the *British Medical Journal* on 21 June 2003 by doctors in London's Institute of Psychiatry (reference Diana Rose and colleagues, BMJ, volume 326, pages 1363-5). They estimated that around 11,000 people in England receive ECT each year. At least one-third of them report significant memory loss after their treatments, but the type of memory loss isn't yet fully determined. The psychiatrist authors of the report concluded that current opinion that the memory loss is not important, and that 80 per cent of patients undergoing ECT were happy with it, is unfounded. They ask for studies that look into patient satisfaction, and the extent of the memory loss, more deeply.

There are always other ways to be helped, and the next few chapters explain them.

Chapter Six

ThinkingThrough Your Depression – What You Can Do forYourself

Cognitive BehaviourTherapy

Treating depression is like the classic sports reporter's description of a football match – it is a game of two halves. Unless you have skipped the previous pages, you have now finished the first half, the one about the biochemistry of depression and its treatment with drugs.

Now you have had your half-time session with the coach, and you are on the field in a very different second half – the half of cognitive behaviour. You will find the two halves very different, but don't be deceived. They are complementary, not alternatives. Most people who embark on cognitive behaviour therapy also need to stay on their drug therapy. When you begin to understand what happens to you, and how your reasoning and feelings change, when you are depressed, it is easier for you to help yourself through the bad periods. That is exactly what cognitive behaviour therapy does.

So let's have a go at explaining depression, not from a biochemical viewpoint, but from a human one.

To start with, cognitive behaviour experts have identified five ways in which we change when we are depressed. Here I must digress a little, and remind you of the book I mentioned earlier – *Overcoming Depression: A Five Areas Approach* by Professor Chris Williams, published byArnold in 2001. It takes the form of a self-help book for people with depression to work through. It is brilliantly laid out in the form of pages of questions and answers for you to tick, and shows many ways in which you can help yourself to a better way of thinking and acting. It is also very self-revealing. Even without depression myself, having gone through the well-planned series of chapters I can see where my own thinking and actions are at fault. It isn't just a book for people with depression, but for anyone who wants to understand himself or herself a bit better. That can only be a good thing. So please get it out of your local library, or better still buy a copy – then ProfessorWilliams will get his just rewards for his authorship!

So back to the five ways in which we change when we are depressed.

First, we all have to face life-shaking problems from time to time. Something hits us out of the blue, like a physical illness in ourselves or our family, or the death of someone close. Or there is a sudden unexpected shift in our financial state, like losing a well-paid job, or our expected pension disappears because of a stock market crash (a very common life event in the early twenty-first century). Or there is a marital disagreement, separation or divorce. Or a family row isolates us: inter-sibling arguments sometimes seem like wars.

How we face up to all these unwanted events depends on the other four aspects of our characters:

- One is what we think. Are our thoughts helpful or unhelpful at such times?
- The second is our emotional response. Do we react in the most appropriate ways (with logic, reason, cool-headedness) when they arise, or do we react with inappropriate emotions such as anger, resentment, suspicion or panic?
- The third is our physical response. Do we get physical symptoms, such as palpitations, breathlessness, indigestion, nausea or diarrhoea?
- The fourth is how we behave. Do we become introverted and withdrawn, or do we become overactive and antisocial? Maybe we start throwing things.

Do you recognize yourself already? If you do, that's a start. Take a little time to think about the way you respond to such 'life events'. Try to stand outside yourself and assess your responses in an unbiased way. Ask yourself three questions:

- How well do I manage unpleasant thoughts or feelings?
- How assertive am I when faced with unwanted events and pressures?
- How good am I at finding practical solutions to my problems?

Then see how you match up with a few common problems.

Let's take an example. You are in the supermarket. You see someone you know in the same aisle. She passes you without stopping to say hello. What is your first reaction? Is it to think that she saw you but pretended not to, because she doesn't like you? Because of that do you feel terrible? Does that then make you cut short your shopping and go home, to be miserable by yourself? And does that make you feel drained, tired, listless and even nauseated and sick? Do you find you have palpitations and then can't get to sleep that night?

This sequence of events may seem laughable to people who have never been depressed. They would simply assume that the other person didn't see them, or was too busy, or perhaps too preoccupied with her own emotional difficulties, to stop to chat. Even if they thought that the other person was really trying to avoid them, they would put the blame for that on the other person and forget it. How would a 'normal' person react to the imagined snub? By going forward and saying hello oneself, breaking any barrier, imagined or real.

However, the sequence is no laughing matter to people who are, or who have been, depressed. They see this behaviour as typical of their own when they are depressed. They remember acting in exactly this way, many times. Analyse what has happened, remembering the five aspects of depression described above.

First there was the problem that you had to face – being ignored, or not noticed in the supermarket by a friend. Look on this as a minor form of that 'life event' mentioned above that stimulates your subsequent thoughts, your mental and physical reactions and behaviour.

Second was your immediate reasoning following the encounter. You assumed a deliberate snub, and blamed yourself for it. That's as negative as you can get! You reacted with suspicion (that you were not liked), with a downturn in mood (misery) and perhaps anger.

Third, your mental reaction created physical distress: tiredness, weakness, 'sick in your stomach', lost appetite, a fast heart rate (palpitations) and sleeplessness.

Fourth, you took inappropriate actions: you cut short your shopping, went home and kept away from other people. You did not want to share your feelings with anyone else.

And all this was because someone you knew failed to acknowledge you in the supermarket. If you could step outside yourself and without bias look at this series of events, you would see how wrong your attitudes and actions are and how much you need to correct them.

That is what cognitive behaviour therapy is all about. It helps you to understand how you think when you are depressed (that's the cognitive part), and then shows you how to change that thinking and your subsequent behaviour accordingly (that's the behaviour part). The good thing about this is that when you do alter your behaviour, your mood lifts. One often follows the other, like day follows night. In fact, that's often how people who manage to change their everyday behaviour describe the change in their depression. One patient described it as 'coming out of the dark into the sunshine'. First comes the behaviour change, then comes the rise in mood.

We can take that supermarket encounter again as an example. Suppose that, instead of thinking the worst, you had gone up to your friend and broken the ice. She might have reacted by apologizing: that morning she had broken her glasses, and most faces were fuzzy to her. She just hadn't recognized you. So you have coffee together, promise to meet up on another shopping day and maybe have lunch. Instead of going home alone, worrying and getting in a physical 'state', you get home in a good mood, looking forward to your next meeting and planning ahead what you might do together. That night you sleep well. No nausea, no weakness, no tiredness, no loss of appetite, no fast heartbeats, no misery. All because you reacted healthily to the 'event'.

So how do you start to change things? The first priority is to examine the types of event that might trigger your depressive reaction. Recognize first of all that no life is without its problems. What you must learn to do is to understand where those problems are for you, and how you can best deal with them.

Problems mainly come under three headings – money, marital and friends, and job worries. We all have them to some extent; an unfortunate few have problems in all these areas, and they can become overwhelming.

Take money first. A recent survey in Britain reported that, on average, people who are in debt owe a sum equivalent to 14 times their monthly income. That rises to 40 times in people on lower incomes in poorer districts. It is not surprising that people with these sorts of financial worries become depressed. If there is no way to increase your income, it is very difficult to see how you can get out of such a debt. Nor is it difficult to understand why they become very depressed.

So, taking the 'five ways' approach, how can you try to resolve your state of mind? The debt is the 'life event'. You react to it negatively, by blaming yourself and feeling miserable. Or you respond with anger, blaming someone else for your predicament (like a partner in a low-paying job). Then you can't sleep, get headaches, feel vaguely sick and argue with people, especially those who are closest to you. And you don't even begin to pay off the debt, so that it mounts, week by week.

Recognize the scenario? It can only be resolved by facing up to it. That means seeking help. There are Citizens' Advice Bureaux (CAB) in every district in Britain. Their counsellors will help you to organize your life by sorting out your repayments and advising on how best to economize on your expenses and outgoings. You will be amazed how just one visit to a CAB counsellor can lift your spirits. Anyone who wants to know how a CAB counsellor can help needs only to watch the programmes put out by BBC television, with Alvin Hall as the money advisor. The series showed just how seriously in debt people can get, and how it destroys their relationships, their self-belief and their peace of mind. Alvin is a great cognitive behaviour therapist, although he may not apply that label to himself.

Let's turn to 'marital' next. You will probably not admit to your doctor or your nurse advisor, and certainly not to your CAB counsellor, that you are having problems with sex. Yet most marriages that founder, founder on that rock. It's assumed that men want sex more often than women, and that for them it is just a physical thing, for self-gratification. Women, so the popular idea goes, need to be wooed, to have some romance, before they can be ready for sex. And they can't become enthusiastic about it if they are tired and anxious after a day of depression and stress.

Yet that isn't necessarily true. Disagreements about sex may come from your loss of sex drive, a common symptom of depression and lack of self-esteem. And that is transmitted to your partner. Problems with sexual relationships between partners are fairly evenly split between the male and female. Depressed men are just as likely to lose their sex drive as their female partners, and this can be a source of frustration for both of them. It can also be a source of anger and resentment, and deteriorating relationships, that can't be solved without professional help.

Does the depression come before the loss of sex drive, or vice versa? It is the old question of the chicken or the egg. Whatever the way round, the answer is to face the problem, just as with all the others, and try to solve it reasonably. Talking about it to your partner is essential, but if that isn't helping, and there are resentments on both sides (there often are), then you need to agree to go together to someone who can help. Sometimes that is your doctor, or a specialist member of the family doctor team. If that isn't comfortable for you both, then an outside counsellor who doesn't know you can help. There is no need for such counsellors to be knowledgeable about the treatment of depression: they are specifically there to help with the sexual problem.

By now you will be realizing that cognitive behaviour therapy is a very practical way of looking at your depression. It looks at your circumstances and your flawed response to them, and tries to correct it. In doing so, it should lift your mood and help you understand yourself more clearly.

So forget your depression for a moment, and think of yourself and how you react to circumstances. Read the following statements, and see how many 'yes' answers you give to them:

- I have frequent arguments with my partner or closest relative
- I can't really talk to them about my problems
- There isn't anyone I can talk to
- I'm always under stress managing my home/partner/children/ dependent parents
- I have debts that I can't see myself ever clearing
- I'm away from my roots and don't like the district I live in
- I don't get on with my neighbours
- I'm having difficulties at work – with colleagues and with keeping up with work demands
- I don't like my job – or I can't get a job and am worried about it

Two or more yeses and you need help.

These are all negative thoughts, suggesting that you are seeing everything from a negative viewpoint. That needs to change – and cognitive behaviour therapy should help you to change it. The next chapter goes into more detail about the kind of negative thoughts you may have, how to recognize when you are thinking negatively, and how to change your thinking.

Chapter Seven

Those Negative Thoughts – and How to Change Them

When you are depressed, the negative is always uppermost. You see, think and interpret things in a bad, rather than a good, way. You blame yourself for not achieving or for anything that has happened to you. How often do you think 'I'm hopeless' or 'I was the one who fouled up that job'? Or you look back on the previous few days and say to yourself that everything that could have gone wrong did so. Or that nothing went to plan. Then you look into the future, and think the worst is bound to happen. For example, asked out by friends, you decline because you don't want to look a fool or be a nuisance. Or you refuse because you think they have only asked you out because they pity you. And anyway, you wouldn't enjoy the occasion. You feel that somehow you will wreck the evening, and it will be your fault and no one else's.

This feeling that others don't really like you pervades all your relationships, with family, friends and workmates. But you wouldn't ever wish to challenge that feeling by trying to find out if this is really so. Feeling that you are not likeable goes along with a feeling that when anything goes badly, you are responsible. You feel under pressure to achieve, and when things go wrong, you take the blame upon yourself, even though, if you look at things rationally, the cause of the problem lies elsewhere. How often have you said to yourself, or to others, 'It's all my fault'?

Finally, there is 'extreme thinking'. There are key words that virtually every person with depression uses a lot. Do you recognize them? They are 'completely', 'total', 'never', 'always' and 'typical'. They seem innocuous words in the right context. But when you use them in describing bad aspects of your everyday life, such as:

- I've been completely useless today
- What a total mess I've made
- I never get things right

- I'm always in the wrong
- That's typical of me, making such a mistake, then you are almost certainly seriously depressed

Non-depressed people realize that nothing is as bad as that. They know that there are reasons for things not turning out quite as well as planned, and that they can't always control them. So they don't blame themselves. They do not have the frank bias against themselves that people with depression show so clearly in their negative thinking. Nor do they feel they need to do things perfectly. Non-depressives understand that people aren't perfect, and that when things go a little awry, it can't be helped. If you are depressed and are set a task, the results of which do quite come up to scratch, then you become very upset, and can't avoid taking the blame yourself.

One example is the dinner hostess who apologizes for her food before anyone has tasted it. She has worked for hours preparing the dinner and, as she puts down the first course, offers the remark that she thinks she has put too much (or too little) salt (or spices, or sauce) in it. Naturally the guests would never have noticed, or have criticized the food in any way – until she brought their attention to it. She has acted as the perfectionist in preparing the meal, and then allowed her bias against herself to come to a head in her self-criticism, at a crucial time when she should be proud of her efforts in front of her friends and family.

Have you done that, or something similar? Then you are showing negative thinking that you need to change.

Here you will probably respond by saying that you can't change the way you think – that it is part of you. That isn't true. This is where behaviour therapy comes into its own. Fundamental to understanding how you can change your thinking is the fact that depression changes your behaviour, as well as your thinking, in a negative and self-harming way. If you consciously change to a more positive and forward-looking pattern of behaviour, no matter how hard it is in the beginning, then your mood will improve, too. You are then well on your way to becoming much less depressed.

Depression affects your behaviour in two direct ways. First, it makes you withdraw into yourself, so that you don't want to do the things you used to find enjoyable, like going out with friends, or pursuing a hobby, or following a particular sporting, social or intellectual interest. Do you recognize that change in yourself?

Second, it makes you choose behaviour that is self-harming, such as drinking excessively, taking illegal drugs, or taking an excess of prescription drugs such as tranquillizers or sleeping tablets. You may be deliberately avoiding other people, workmates, friends or family. You may not be eating regularly, and may have stopped cooking for yourself. You may even have started to injure yourself – for example, made a few tentative cuts with a knife on your arms. Any of these patterns of behaviour are signs of serious depression.

Ask yourself if you have started to behave in any of these ways. Have you stopped calling your parents or children, or brothers or sisters? Do you spend most of your leisure time at home alone? Do you eat alone at work? Has it been a long time since you initiated a visit to an old friend?

Are you abusing alcohol or other drugs? Are you suspicious of other people? Are you more demanding than you were? Do you always believe you will fail in everything you do? Do you think others are about to let you down or ignore or reject you? Are you getting deeper into debt because you are trying to buy yourself out of depression?

If you recognize that these are typical of your life, you need to change because you are now in a vicious downward spiral: the more negative your behaviour becomes, the deeper your depression becomes. You absolutely must change your behaviour if you want to become better. Antidepressant drugs alone will not do that for you.

So how can you help yourself?

First, recognize that you can't beat your depression alone. Left to your own devices, you will probably just get worse. You need to talk to a trusted and good friend about how you feel, and ask for his or her support. That's particularly important when you get into one of your blacker moods, but you need to see your friends regularly, regardless of your mood. Your friends want to see you in your good times, as well as your bad ones. That makes it easier for them to help you.

The same goes for seeing your doctor or community nurse. Make regular appointments and don't miss them. You need an outsider, preferably a trusted professional, to assess your moods and to take any action they feel is needed to keep you healthy. You also need to be boosted in your better days as well as your bad ones.

Just as important, keep up your interests. You may feel less enthusiastic than you were about things, but don't let that feeling stop you taking part in social activities even if, at the start, you feel suspicious, inferior, guilty or useless. It's better to have a hobby that takes you out of the home and into meeting people than to have one that involves you being home alone, when all that can happen is that all these feelings will deepen.

It is worth repeating here that all these changes in your behaviour are usually accompanied by physical changes, too. Depression isn't just a problem with thought and mood, it is reflected in a slowing of many of the body's physical processes, too. So you feel tired all the time and don't seem to be able to rouse yourself into physical activity. Even getting dressed in the morning becomes a debilitating chore, and travelling to work exhausts you. Although I will be heavily criticized for suggesting this, many people with 'ME' or 'post-viral fatigue syndrome' or 'chronic fatigue syndrome' (all different descriptions of a similar chronic debilitating illness that has caught the public interest in recent years) are, in fact, suffering from depression.

You may not bother to cook and eat regularly, and therefore lose weight. But you may also 'comfort eat', nibbling at snacks throughout the day and even night, so that your weight escalates. That, obviously, makes you more depressed.

Your gut slows along with the depression, so that you become constipated. You can help that by eating plenty of fibre and fruit and drinking lots of water through the day, but the main help to constipation is regular physical exercise. If you keep your stomach muscles in good trim, your constipation is much more easily eradicated.

Depression also makes you more stressed and tense than usual. So, although you are less physically active and tired all the time, you still may be restless and agitated. You can't feel comfortable in any one position for any length of time, so you fidget and fuss, which makes it difficult for anyone around you to cope. The tension may be so bad that it gives you a headache, stemming from cramp in the two big neck muscles at the base of the back of the head, that extends through the scalp into your upper eyebrows. 'Tension headache' like this is a very common symptom of depression, and is well known to family doctors as perhaps 'flagging up' a case of hidden depression.

The tension may be translated into the gut muscles. That can lead to irritable bowel, another collection of symptoms that has gained prominence in recent years, along with ME. Cramp in the gut muscles gives colicky pains, and can make you feel bloated and disturb your normal bowel habit. The commonest bowel disturbance is the passing of showers of small 'rabbity' pellets, that some people describe as constipation, and others, curiously, describe as diarrhoea! But alternate bouts of constipation and diarrhoea are also a sign of irritable bowel, and of depression. Treating irritable bowel with antidepressant drugs can often be as successful as giving drugs specifically to relieve bowel cramps.

Other physical disturbances that appear with depression include dyspepsia – or 'indigestion' or an 'upset stomach' – which causes pains in the upper abdomen related to meals or to hunger. When these are investigated, it is usual to find no real problem. Such patients usually do not have ulcers or hiatus hernias, the common causes of dyspepsia which are unrelated to depression.

Depression can also cause chest pains that can be mistaken for angina. True angina is a pain due to narrowing of the coronary arteries that supply the heart muscle with blood. In chest pains related to depression, just like those related to dyspepsia, all investigations have negative results, leaving the doctor and patient in a quandary over what to do. The real cure is to be found in lifting the depression, and not in prescribing drugs to relieve 'heart' pain.

Chapter Eight

Your Changed Mood when Depressed
– How it Affects You

'Feeling' is quite different from 'thinking'. In the last chapter I described how, when you are depressed, you think negatively and even develop negative physical symptoms. These are things that you can do something about. It's more difficult to be able to do something about the way you feel. A major aspect of depression is a constant low 'mood' – the way that you feel, within yourself. We have so many words to describe a low mood, and you will recognize the one you use most often yourself. Few people actually use the word 'depressed' themselves to describe their mood, but what about feeling 'blue', 'low', 'sad', 'down' or (possibly the commonest) just 'fed up'?

These words are so often used in conversation that they are looked on almost as normal states of mind, to describe occasional instances of reactions to problems experienced in the normal routine of life. It is when you are using them, yourself, to describe your moods, day in, day out, that they are clearly euphemisms for depression. Do you use them to describe your mood several times a week? Then you probably need help.

There are other pointers to a low mood that is clearly part of a depressive illness, rather than a normal reaction to life's circumstances. Mood that is low each morning and lifts during the day is one. If that is a regular pattern, then you may well have an underlying depression.

Another pointer is loss of enjoyment in the things you used to love doing. Maybe you had a hobby or sport that took up a lot of your leisure time – and now you can't be bothered with it. Those Saturday afternoons at the match, or evenings out with the girls, now hold no anticipation for you. The enthusiasm for doing things or meeting people has fizzled out. It's not that you actively now dislike doing these things: instead, you just feel no emotion about them. You enjoy nothing, and you feel no emotional reaction to anything, good or bad. If you have got to this stage, you really need professional help, fast.

Yet another mood change is a habit of feeling guilty about anything you do, or have omitted to do. You feel that you are letting others down all the time. You may even feel that you are offending against some moral or ethical code, a feeling that would astonish others if you shared it with them. This type of feeling is also a mood change, not a change in your character. A constant feeling of guilt can really destroy you: it must be brought out into the open and tackled head on.

On top of guilt there are worry and anxiety. The two words are interchangeable, though most people would equate worry with quietly, inwardly, going over a seemingly insoluble problem again and again, and anxiety with showing your worry in the form of outward stress – picking over a problem again and again with other people and building up obvious tension as you do so. Neither is helpful, because you can't solve a problem simply by constantly turning it over in your mind, whether you do it outwardly or inwardly.

The next step onwards from worry and anxiety is panic. That's a feeling of real fear, even terror. In panic you really do feel that something overwhelmingly awful is about to happen to you, and that you can do nothing about it. It makes you lose your ability to reason through your problem: your heart races, you become breathless and you want to hide away from whatever is threatening you. Although panic attacks are extremely unpleasant, they are not life-threatening, despite many people thinking that they are.

Other examples of changed mood in depression are anger and irritability. You get angry and annoyed at the slightest thing – perhaps as simple as a partner leaving a door open or something on the floor. Tiny everyday things that could be put right in a couple of minutes become big things that you go on about for hours, distressing yourself and everyone around you. Anger is such a wasted emotion, and one that can destroy relationships because it isn't one to which other people find it easy to be sympathetic.

After the outburst of anger you may react with embarrassment or shame. You feel that you have lost control and become ashamed of having done so. You may feel inferior or that others are judging you, justifiably, as having let them down.

From that feeling can come others about the people around you. The most destructive is that you become suspicious about them. You begin to think they are talking behind your back, or are plotting against you. That feeling can extend to the people closest to you, such as a spouse or parent or child. Taking that to extremes, you may lose all faith in everyone's feelings towards you, and withdraw from all of them. This happens just at the time when you need most support from them, and is why you don't seek that support and sympathy. This is paranoia, and is a very severe sign of depression.

Now go over this chapter again. Do you recognize your own feelings in it? How often have you in the past week or so felt:

- 'blue' or 'low'
- lowest in the mornings, and better in the evenings
- no real pleasure in things you used to enjoy
- no feelings, joyful or sorrowful, at all
- guilty
- worried or anxious
- panic
- angry
- irritable
- ashamed
- suspicious

If any of these are regular feelings, then you need to change. How to change is the subject of the next chapter.

Chapter Nine

Using Cognitive Behaviour to Change Yourself: Changing Your Situation

By now you will have recognized that you have a lot to change – remember the five areas of depression:

- the situation (for want of a better word) in which you find yourself
- your negative thinking
- your lowered mood and feelings
- your wrong behaviour
- your physical symptoms

Looking at your depression in this way you may feel that what you need to do is too much, even overwhelming. You can't change them all at once, so you don't find a way of changing any of them. It's best to try to change things one at a time.

We will start with your 'situation'. Let's go back to the financial problem. You are in debt, and can't see a way out of it. You need to take action on it, regardless of whether you are depressed or not. But if you are depressed, you are more likely than not to take no action, as if the debt will vanish by itself. Obviously it won't, and that ultimately will make you more depressed. Taking positive action may not entirely lift your depression, but it will make it more bearable.

So what to do? Group sessions in cognitive behaviour therapy would 'brainstorm' the problem. Each member of the group will toss in an answer, no matter how ridiculous. For example, you could rob a bank or mug someone – but that would bring more problems. Or you could switch your debt between different credit cards – but that would only worsen the problem in the long run. Or you could pay off the minimum each week and just keep your head above water. Or you could re-negotiate your loan, with the benefit of a counsellor, such as someone at the Citizens' Advice Bureau (CAB).

You might even be brave enough to go to your bank and ask for an overdraft to pay it off. You may need someone to come with you, to help in the negotiations, but you must be the one who takes the lead.

Whichever sensible solution you come up with (I assume you are not a criminal), you will feel better after taking the plunge and sorting something out. And that's a start towards feeling better. You have had some cognition into your problem, and you are behaving in the way that may help solve it.

Suppose you now go to the bank. Being depressed, you will naturally look on the down side of things. You expect the person you will be dealing with will be severe, judgemental, maybe bullying, certainly looking on you as inferior. The thought of approaching him or her frightens and depresses you further.

Once in the office, however, you find the bank staff pleasant, understanding, smiling, polite and helpful. Your problem is analysed in a kindly but professional way, and you leave with a plan for the future that will mean a way to reduce and eventually eradicate your debt. You now have shed a huge burden from your shoulders. Your mood will lift, and the therapy has begun.

Let's take another example. You are a young mother with three children. Your husband is a hard-working self-employed professional – maybe a lawyer or a doctor. You always seem to be alone with the children, struggling to keep on top of things, while your husband is out all hours. When he comes home, all he wants to do is snooze in front of the television. You can't remember when you last went out together. You are both too tired to make love when you finally get to bed at night. You feel that you are growing apart. You are even beginning to suspect that he has someone at the office (or at the surgery) who is taking your place.

It's a very familiar story for thirty- to forty-something couples. When the man is at the height of his earning powers and the woman feels trapped by caring for the children, depression can hit hard.

So what can you do? Let's try the brainstorming again. You can kill him – but that's a bit drastic and won't solve your problem. Being behind bars for the rest of the time your children are growing up won't help your depression. You could sulk and do nothing, and fall into a deeper depression. That will just make matters worse in the long run. You could drive down to the office on one of his late nights in the hope of catching him with the imagined fancy woman. That's

74

bad on two counts. If he hasn't another woman, then he will be very upset at your suspicions. And your appearance at the office would not be helpful if the reason for it became obvious to the other staff. It would further sour relations, rather than improve them.

Then there's the 'let's have it out' row at home, with raised voices and things you regret saying afterwards. Perhaps in front of the children – and that won't be good for their relationships with either you or their father.

How about preparing a special meal – the one he really likes – for him arriving home one evening, after farming out the kids to a friend for the night? And as you eat, discuss in a quiet and pleasant manner ways in which you can make your home life better? It's worth a shot. Arrange to do the same (or to go out for dinner, or to a movie or the theatre) regularly, on evenings when there are no pressures on either of you. Even if you feel depressed, make an effort to fulfil your part of the bargain. Make it the most important part of your time together. After a while, you will find that your mood is lifting, and you have something enjoyable to look forward to again. As with the solution to the debt problem, taking action to change your 'situation' leads to a lift in your depression. Cognition leads to behaviour change, and that leads to a lightened mood.

These are only two common examples of the many situations in which people find themselves trapped. If you look at your life in detail, there are probably several 'situations' that you could manage better. Maybe your relationships with your parents or your children need attention. Have things been said that shouldn't have? Or have you not done things that, on reflection, you should have? What about deciding to put them right? If you don't, they will keep on eating away at you, and your depression hasn't a chance of lifting, even with the most powerful drugs.

Having started to take actions, now is the time to change your way of thinking. Remember that the second aspect of depression is negative thinking, mainly about yourself. It is time to change from being a passive observer of other people's lives to become an assertive person in your own right. That's what the next chapter is about.

Chapter Ten

Changing Yourself: Changing Your Negative Thinking – Becoming Assertive

Remember the five aspects of depression from the previous chapter? The second was negative thinking. You must become less negative and more assertive. Be clear about what 'assertive' means. It is simply sticking up for yourself. It doesn't mean 'aggressive' or 'rude'. But it does mean changing from your usual negative thoughts about yourself (and you must admit you have them) to a more positive approach.

Let's take a few examples. You go into a shop, and the assistant doesn't make an effort to help you. She may ignore you, or not show the slightest interest in your custom. Your normal reaction would perhaps be to slink away, or to wait patiently (though unhappily) until she notices you. You are being made to feel small, or even non-existent. But you are not non-existent. You are you, and a customer. The assistant should be doing her utmost to help you. So you may as well firmly remind her of that. Go up to her, even if she is talking to another shop assistant, and ask her for what you want. It isn't rude or impolite to do so – it is her responsibility to serve you, and not yours to wait upon her whim.

By doing this you are showing positive, not negative thinking. And when the assistant responds by being extra helpful (because she probably realizes she was in the wrong – there's every chance she is depressed, too), you will feel better about yourself. It is a little triumph for you that you can savour. And in doing so, you may lift your mood, even if only slightly. From these little acorns, oak trees of self-confidence can grow.

Take a more personal relationship. Say a friend has borrowed something from you. It could be a favourite book, or some garden shears, or something to do with the house. It may not be anything expensive or even important, but to have it back matters to you. Your friend has not brought it back, and it never crops up in conversation.

You haven't wanted to create a fuss, and so you have lapsed into the negative thinking of doing nothing about it. That depresses you further and, inside you (because you would obviously not admit it to your friend), the fact that you are not going to get it back is souring your relationship. If you are depressed, that souring can quickly deepen your depression.

What is the answer? It would be simple for anyone who is not depressed. They would have no qualms about asking for the object back. You find the thought of this very difficult. But once you have done it, you will find that its prompt return, along with a probable apology, will not only have cleared the air and improved your friendship, but will also have lightened your mood.

Maybe you have trouble at work. Your boss has put pressure on you. Perhaps you have been expected to do too much and are getting only brickbats as a reward. How do you normally respond? By keeping your head down, suffering in silence, and taking your negative thoughts home with you, to unburden them on your family. But you take no action, because you think your very livelihood is at stake. Not only that, but, because you seem to be failing in your work, you may even feel that anyone could do it better and more efficiently than you – and that deepens your depression further.

It is no use responding to this with your own anger or anxiety. What you must do, as in the cases above, is to be assertive. Take the bull(y) by the horns and confront him or her. But do it very professionally. Coolly and calmly ask for time for a discussion on your work, how much you can do in the time allotted to it, and even bring in your colleague's reaction to you. Show that it is unfair and incorrect in the work environment, but do so without implying criticism. No matter what reaction you receive, you will feel better as you clear the air and it dawns on you that you are as important as anyone else in the workplace, and that your rights must be respected.

In all these examples you have replaced negative thoughts with positive ones. You have replaced 'passive' behaviour with 'assertive' behaviour. And in doing so, you will have improved your self-esteem. That is a big step towards lifting your depression.

Let's examine the difference between passive and assertive thoughts and behaviour.

People who behave passively hide their thoughts and feelings, nursing them inside and worrying over them constantly. They look on other people's needs as more important than their own, so that they buckle under every time there is a conflict of interest. They feel that other people have rights and privileges that they don't. They don't think they have much to contribute, so they stay silent and let other people make all the decisions. They may even not wish to contribute to a conversation or voice their own opinions because they fear ridicule. In a word, because they always want to please others, they avoid all conflict at all times.

Passive behaviour patterns like those in the last paragraph are comforting in the short term. They help people avoid arguments and confrontations that they fear will be unpleasant. So they reduce anxiety and at the same time give them a self-satisfying feeling of 'martyrdom'. But in the long run, behaving passively lowers your self-esteem to zero and causes stress, internalized anger and a deeper and deeper depression.

Do you recognize yourself in the last two paragraphs? Then you have an urgent need to become more assertive. Just by doing that, you will change your life for the better.

However, don't make the mistake of becoming 'aggressive' rather than 'assertive'. Aggressive behaviour is demanding and angry. You feel that your needs are above those of others. You have more to contribute than they have, and in demanding your rights you trample all over the rights of others. You blame your anger on the faults of others. In the short run, you feel much better, but as you continue with your aggressive behaviour you become guilty and ashamed of what you are doing. You make whoever you are aggressive towards, work colleagues or family, dislike you. And in the long run, your self-esteem falls steeply and the depression continues to deepen.

Assertiveness isn't about winning an argument against others. It is about expressing your feelings in an open way that is honest and appropriate, but not demanding. You wish to let people know that your needs are important, and that if they are not met, you will feel worthless and unhappy. When you ask for your rights, you do so in a way that does not affect the rights of others. You, and the people around you, get to know that you, like all of them, have something special to contribute to your mutual happiness and benefit.

In making these changes, you will become more confident in yourself, and that growing self-confidence will surely lift your low mood. Your new self-knowledge (i.e. cognition) brings about a new behaviour pattern that will help to lift your depression. We keep returning to the principle of cognitive behaviour therapy – with better knowledge of yourself, you can change your behaviour, and that will go a long way to lifting your depression.

Professor Chris Williams, in his excellent book, sets out the rules of assertion. I can't better them. They are listed here:

1   Respect myself – who I am and what I do
2   Recognize my own needs as an individual (apart from my role as a spouse or parent)
3   Make clear 'I' statements about how I feel and think – so that I am prepared to disagree, politely but firmly, with other people's decisions
4   Allow myself to make mistakes – that is a normal part of life
5   Change my mind if I wish to
6   Ask for 'thinking over' time – so that when asked to do something, I can have time to mull it over
7   Allow myself to be pleased with what I have done, and share the pleasure with others
8   Ask for what I want, rather than wait for someone else to notice it
9   Recognize that I am not responsible for the behaviour of other adults
10 Respect other people's right to be assertive, and that they must expect the same in return from me

Of course, it is all very well to lay down the rules. It is more difficult to stick to them. So cognitive behaviour therapists have developed techniques to help you to develop your assertiveness. One is what Dr Williams calls the 'broken record' system. Say you wish to put right what you see as a misunderstanding or an error by a friend. Before you meet or call, you learn what you are going to say, much as actors learn their lines. Then you are not put off by any reply or response. If there is some argument, just repeat your point of view, so that the phrases recur again and again, like a crack in a record. Once you have said what you meant to say, you will feel much more relaxed and confident in yourself.

Let's take an example. You are having a difficult time at work. You are a graphic designer, and it is your job to be involved in any graphics work that your company needs to produce. You find that one of the managers has been farming out work to outside companies, without informing you. This is undermining your status and your confidence, and you feel that you are being undervalued. Ordinarily, you would keep quiet and complain to your long-suffering partner when you get home. This is negative thinking. Instead, you should try the following approach. The conversation should go something like this:

You: Can I have a quiet word, please?

Manager: Sure, by all means. What is it about?

You: I really value my position as graphic designer in the company, and want to make sure that we both agree on how I can be used to the greatest benefit of everyone in it. I hear that you have gone outside for one of your projects. Is that true?

Manager: Well, yes, but I didn't think it would upset you. I thought that it would help ease your workload.

You: All it does is suggest to me that you don't value me or trust me. If you want to handle a graphic design project you should at least let me or one of my staff know what you are planning, and invite us to make suggestions or comments. And you should use me first if you can.

Manager: I'm sorry if you feel that way. However, I must have the choice to go outside if I want to.

You: I have to repeat that with all projects that need graphic design, you should at least come to me first. I am very uncomfortable with the idea that such projects are going outside without your in-house team being involved and asked if they can help. This is not the way a management team should work. By going outside you are undermining the morale of your staff.

Manager:	Right. Maybe I don't know enough about what you can do and what is available in house. Can we arrange a longer meeting at a time convenient to both of us, so that we can straighten out our differences?
You:	That will be fine. But in the meantime, can we be asked to compete against that outside design team that you are thinking of commissioning now? That way you will be showing good faith.
Manager:	I will send the material to you today.
You:	And I would like you to make a commitment that you will come to us for your graphic design needs before going outside the company.
Manager:	You have made your point. Let's arrange that meeting now, so that we can come to an agreement on that point and on any others you wish to raise.

The result of your assertiveness and openness is a new undertstanding with your manager, and a better feeling for you about your worth and standing with your working colleagues. That will help your mood – and maybe present a different 'you' to your colleagues that they haven't seen before. Your mood, as a consequence of your assertive behaviour, will lighten. And you will go home and talk about your minor triumph at work, rather than your misery at being overlooked.

Let's take another example. You are the mother of a 14-year-old girl, who wants to go out to a late-night party with her friends. You aren't happy with this, as you suspect that there will be alcoholic drink and maybe even drugs, and there will be little adult supervision. So you want to say 'no'. Normally you find that very difficult, and can be easily persuaded by your daughter to give in. So while she is at the party, you sit at home worrying and becoming more depressed. There is another way – by using your assertiveness. The conversation between you and your daughter could go like this:

Daughter:	Can I go to the party tonight, mum?
You:	No. I've decided you are too young, and that you are at too much risk from the people you meet there. So I'm using a mother's prerogative for a 14-year-old, and saying 'no'. Ask a few friends round here if you want to have some fun.
Daughter:	But that's not fair. All my mates will be there, and I know how to take care of myself.
You:	No. Fairness doesn't come into it. It's my decision as a responsible parent to make decisions for you, and I say 'no'. I do not want you exposed at 14 to risks of alcohol and drugs, and you are too young to protect yourself.
Daughter:	You don't trust me, and all the other parents will let their daughters go. I'm not a child any more.
You:	It's not that I don't trust you. But I don't trust other people around you, and I have to take responsibility for you and what happens to you. So you must respect my decision to say 'no'. I'm not apologizing to you for taking that decision, and you must understand that you must be older and more mature before you can go to parties like this. That's my final answer. As for other parents, they must make their own decisions. I must be allowed to make mine on your behalf without you putting pressure on me and using them to bully me into changing my mind. You are still a child, and I am responsible for you. So the answer is a firm and definite 'no'.
Daughter:	I think you are horrible. You are ruining my life.
You:	That's a bit over the top. I find it difficult to say 'no' to you because you are my daughter, and we are so

close. But there are times when it is important for you to understand that I have a right to say 'no' to you, and that I don't need to apologize or to elaborate on my reasons for doing so. And if you respond by rudeness, it will make things worse between us. I would prefer that you accept my decisions in the same spirit as I am showing to you. We need to be honest and open towards each other, and to respect each other's feelings. Then we will get along together just fine in the future.

Daughter: Sorry, mum. I want that, too. I'll stay in tonight.

If you have teenage children you may think that conversation ended rather too well – but it can happen. Probably the most important aspect of assertiveness is finding a way to say 'no' to a friend or close family member. Most people find it very difficult to say 'no'. If you are depressed, and have low self-esteem, it is even more difficult than usual because you don't trust your own judgement. You think other people, even your 14-year-old daughter, have more rights to make decisions than you, even if you disagree fundamentally with them. You don't want to be looked upon as selfish or mean, and you don't want to be rejected by them, so you acquiesce in decisions to which you are actually opposed. You may feel that you will be loved less by them if you oppose their wishes. That is classical negative thinking, and can only lead to long-term deepening of your depression.

Being able to say 'no' is not selfish or rude or hostile. As in the conversation above, it can be helpful and kindest in the long run. And there are ways to say it that don't need to seem rude and unfriendly. The rules about saying 'no' are simple. Say it in an honest way, but not rudely. Do say that you are uncomfortable in saying 'no', that you do not find it easy. But don't apologize for doing so. You have every right to say 'no' to anyone, if that is your decision, and it is wrong for anyone else to try to bully or coerce you into saying 'yes'. If you say 'yes' when you would rather say 'no', it will only lead to feelings of resentment and, if you are depressed, it can only make the depression worse.

Chapter Eleven

Changing Yourself:
Changing Unhelpful 'Extreme'
Thinking

Chapter 10 described negative thinking and how to change that by becoming assertive. However, patterns of thinking in depression can go well beyond simple negative thoughts. You can descend into a vicious spiral of what the cognitive behaviour experts define as 'extreme' thinking. Once in this thinking mode, every thought you have reinforces your view of yourself as worthless. If you are depressed, you will surely recognize the ways of extreme thinking described here. I have touched on them in a previous chapter, but here they are in more detail.

There are six examples of extreme thinking that are features of depression. You will almost certainly recognize them as ways in which you often think.

The first is to be biased against yourself in the way you think. For example, when you assess your strengths and weaknesses, you play up your weaknesses and play down your strengths. You forget your best achievements and emphasize your failures.

The second is always to look on the black side. In any plan, you always look at the possible drawbacks, and underestimate the probable benefits.

The third is that you think the future is awful for you in particular. You are certain that, whatever you do, things that can go wrong will go wrong. A small but very common example of this is to read the leaflet for the drugs you have been prescribed and to be certain that you will develop many, if not all, of the side effects listed there. You can't be convinced that side effects are rare and tiny compared to the benefits.

Fourth, you 'read the minds' of everyone around you. You are always trying to assess what they are thinking of you, and you always conclude that they don't like you, or at best don't care about you.

Fifth, you always take personal responsibility for anything that goes wrong around you, even though to others it is palpably obvious that you have not been to blame. That goes for things going right, too. If you give a party, you feel that it's your role to make sure that everyone is having a great time – despite the fact that people make their own pleasure. Once the ice has been broken, you don't have to go on trying to entertain – your guests can entertain each other, and you can relax. Does that thought make you feel guilty? Then you are thinking negatively, and even extremely. Let go, and relax instead.

Last, when you are thinking about, or organizing, what you do, you make absolute rules for yourself. You constantly use words like 'never' and 'always' when you are talking about what you do, and you make rules about your everyday life that involve words like 'must' and 'got to'.

Extreme thinking like this may initially be the result of a depressed mood, but it is also the cause of further depression, so if you indulge in it you will descend into that spiral of ever-worsening depression that was mentioned in the last chapter.

Let's take an example of the sort of extreme thinking that can deepen a depressed mood. You are a young artist, trying to make her way as a professional modern painter. You have graduated from art college with a good degree, and you are struggling to get recognized. You have to create a portfolio of paintings for an exhibition that a friendly dealer has arranged for you. The deadline for the paintings to be delivered to the gallery is drawing closer, but you are behind with them. Somehow, you can never get the final result absolutely right. There always seems to be something more that needs to be added, or some line or stroke that has to be reduced or re-painted. You spend a lot of time making each picture perfect, so that none of them is, in your eyes, what you want it to be.

Looking at your paintings, you feel that you are a failure. They are not good enough to put in front of the discerning public – prospective buyers, you think, will not like them, and may even ridicule them. You want to throw them away.

This is no fiction: it is a story of artists that has been common for centuries. But it is a good example of extreme thinking – of bias against yourself. You have a negative view of yourself. You think your future is bleak because no one will buy your paintings. You think others will reject them (the 'mind reading' mentioned earlier). And you think it is all your fault. You will never be good enough to be a professional artist.

Remember that it is the depressed mood that is producing all these extreme thoughts. They, in turn, will further depress you. You have to change your thoughts and actions to break the vicious downward spiral.

How can you do that? First of all you become assertive. You have faith in your ability to paint and declare your pictures finished. You do no more work on them, and you present them as complete works of art. You ask your gallery owner and some trusted friends to see them. They make favourable comments on them and congratulate you, and agree to help you organize the exhibition.

Of course your first thought, with your negativity, is to believe that they are just being kind and that they don't really appreciate your art. Again, this is your extreme thinking getting in the way. You must listen to them, trust them and go ahead with the show, no matter how low you feel inside. On the first day of the show, you sell a few paintings – making enough to pay off the gallery owner and to buy your groceries and pay your rent. You are on the way. Your morale is boosted and you feel better. No matter by how small an amount, your depression has started to lift. You can get on with painting the pictures for your next exhibition, knowing that you have a growing clientele for your work.

Of course, such thinking applies to everything you do. It applies to your thoughts about work, your relationships with others, and your closest friendships. Whenever you start thinking in this extreme way, you must recognize the thought for what it is – a manifestation of your depression. It may enter your head, but you have to cast it out again, quickly, and replace it with another that is much more helpful.

For example, you may not sell a painting for a week or more. You may start thinking that you are the rotten artist that you previously thought you were, and that you will never sell another one. Banish this reasoning at once. Positively throw it out and replace it with a much more helpful one, such as: 'I've got a good training, I have already proven my worth, I don't have anything to prove to anyone, and I will start selling again.' Don't blame yourself for a temporary 'blip' in your fortunes, but take steps to put them right. For example, talk to other gallery owners to see if you can exhibit with them. Get friends and people who have bought your work to help publicize it.

Take marketing advice on how best to sell paintings, and to whom, in your district and further afield. Get involved in the business of marketing your materials, as well as actually painting. Before you know what has hit you, you could well be on a roll and your depression will have vanished along with your anonymity.

I've used our young painter friend as an example, but her story can be repeated in any walk of life. Anyone with depression may show this pattern of extreme thinking and can take appropriate actions to change it. It is a question of looking at yourself and avoiding the six pitfalls:

1   Don't be biased against yourself – don't judge yourself harshly
2   Don't keep having a negative view of things
3   Don't think the future is all bad
4   Don't keep trying to guess what others think about you – you will
    almost always be wrong
5   Don't take the responsibility for absolutely everything that
    happens around you – recognize that things that go wrong may
    be someone else's fault
6   . Don't think in extremes, in that you don't constantly use words
    like always, must, never, ought and should

Things don't always go to plan; just accept that they don't need to. Relax, and you will feel brighter.

Part of this extreme thought pattern spills over into your behaviour. Because people with depression think so negatively, they often withdraw into themselves. They don't want to meet people, even close friends and immediate family. Along with shedding the negative and extreme thoughts, you have to shed that behaviour, too. This is dealt with in the next chapter.

Chapter Twelve

Changing Yourself: Becoming More Outward Going

Having read thus far, you will have recognized in yourself many of the facets of depression that show themselves in changes in your way of thinking and in your mood. If that is so, you will surely recognize in yourself the behaviour pattern described in this chapter – a reduction in your physical activity. Virtually universally present in depression is a sense that you want to withdraw away from society.

Prime Minister Margaret Thatcher once famously stated that 'there is no such thing as society'. She could not have been more wrong. To recover from depression it is essential that you feel at home and comfortable with the people around you – to be included in normal society. Without a good relationship with the people you meet every day it is impossible to feel good in yourself. Feeling good in yourself is precisely what is absent when you are depressed.

In depression you lose all sense of pleasure in the things you used to enjoy doing. You stop going out with friends, or taking pleasure in hobbies, or even reading quietly at home. Nothing gives you that sense of pleasure that was a normal part of your life before depression hit.

As if that weren't enough, you may even start to do self-destructive things that you would not have dreamt of when you were well. You may turn to alcohol. Alcoholism is a strong pointer to depression. You may become excessively dependent on your friends and family for things that were no bother for you to do on your own before the illness. For example you may not eat properly or launder your clothes regularly. Your appearance may deteriorate, and friends will notice that you are not as fresh or tidy as you were. You may go on a spending spree, in a subconscious effort to buy yourself out of your depression. That may lead to money management problems that will, in the long run, deepen your depression.

Along with these changes in behaviour, you can't be bothered to do things, and make the excuse that you are 'tired all the time'. Even when you manage to achieve something, you gain no enjoyment from it. Your negative thinking is accompanied by a loss of enthusiasm for any activity. You get to thinking that the whole business of day-to-day living is just too much effort.

As the depression deepens further, you don't want any contact with anyone. You leave the phone unanswered or even disconnect it. When people call, you stay in a back room and don't answer the door. Even those essential jobs around the house, like mending a tap or cleaning the toilet or simply making the bed, are left undone. The house becomes untidy and, frankly, a tip.

How do you make the change that will help raise your mood? You can't change everything at the same time. You may even have tried to do so, and found the effort impossible. It is better to make small changes first – ones that you know you can do with only a little effort on your own part. So change one 'down' aspect of your life first, leaving all the others for the moment unchanged.

Which one do you change? That's up to you. One way to make the decision is to make a list of the ways in which you are behaving in a way that is unhelpful to you, and choose one that you can feel you can change for the better without too much effort on your part.

Take, for example, the fact that you have been avoiding people for a long time. Why not ask someone around? Not necessarily for a meal, but for a cup of tea and a chat. Choose someone really close, such as a sister or a very close, long-time friend. Someone you know will welcome the call and will not be surprised by its coming out of the blue after a long time of silence from you. That's a start. Take the change bit by bit. You may arrange to meet again, regularly, or just to phone each other at a pre-arranged time every day – something to keep the social contact going.

Don't try to do big things to begin with. For example, don't ask a lot of people round: the organization will be more difficult, take up more time and just give you more worries. There are two crucial criteria for these first steps back to normal relationships: you should be able to achieve them without too much preparation and hassle, and they should help you in that they are likely to raise your mood. So preferably invite someone you know has a sense of humour and won't dwell on health matters, particularly depression!

Of course, making that first call won't be easy. You will worry that the person you are about to call will ask a lot of questions, or think badly of you for not getting in touch before. You may even be 'mind reading' her thoughts (remember from the previous chapter that this is one of the problems with depression).

Nevertheless, you make the first phone call. Unfortunately she is out, and there is no reply. Don't let this first obstacle stop your resolve. Try again, or leave a message on the answerphone. Keep phoning until you can talk, and arrange to meet on a particular day, at a specific time and place. Even though you still worry about the meeting, don't succumb to the temptation to cancel or postpone it. When you do meet, you may be surprised how much you enjoy it and how much you look forward to the next time. From then on, you are helping your depression to lift.

That's when you can start to tackle the next type of problem behaviour. You could tackle the housework that you have neglected. Or get back to that hobby you dropped, or the sport for which you lost your enthusiasm. You can get back to cooking and eating properly, enjoying good meals, rather than neglecting yourself. If you have been drinking too much, you can, with the help of trusted friends, ration it. Don't try to make all these changes at the same time. Resolve to tackle one at a time, over a long period.

When you do so, don't make impossible demands upon yourself. For example, don't try to clean up the whole house. Just aim to clean up one room, and don't think of the next until you have done it. Don't come off alcohol altogether: you probably won't keep it up, and when you backslide you will be plunged into a deeper depression. Instead, just savour one drink slowly, and take a non-alcoholic drink of juice or water in between each alcoholic one. Spread out your drinks, and make the number of drinks you have each day realistically lower than before. Have a friend you can phone to come to see you if you realize you are being tempted to drink too much. Do take this advice about alcohol seriously. Drinking too much is so often a very important part of depression that the next chapter is devoted to it and how you can overcome your need for it.

Then be happy that you are slowly improving the quality of your life as you tackle each problem behaviour. You can even measure the improvement every day. Start a diary in which you record each evening all the good things that have happened during the day – everything that you found gave you pleasure or a sense of achievement. They may be thoughts about someone you met, or something you completed at work, or even just a conversation you had, or a television or radio programme you enjoyed. Take time, before you go to bed, to look back on them with a sense of satisfaction that things are going better. Don't record the bad thoughts, the ones that pulled you down a little. The diary can become part of your 'therapy', something you can look forward to writing each evening and look back upon later. After a month or two, when you look back on what you wrote, you may be pleasantly surprised by how your life has improved, in all sorts of ways.

Chapter Thirteen

Changing Yourself: Alcohol and Drugs

If you are depressed, alcohol doesn't help. Alcohol has a reputation for being a 'pick me up'. It's thought to calm the troubled mind, and many of us look forward to a small drink at the end of a hard day. For anyone who is depressed, unfortunately, that small drink becomes a large one, then two, then more. And alcohol in these amounts directly depresses you.

So here are the facts about alcohol.

Drinking more than the minimum each day both depresses you and delays any reversal of depression by drugs or by cognitive behaviour therapy. It increases panic attacks, makes them worse and makes them last longer. If you get drunk, you become confused and even violent. Afterwards there is the usual remorse and deeper depression. Alcohol heightens your suspicion of other people, even causing you to become paranoid. It is addictive, with all that means about the need to take more of it day by day, and cravings for it when you go without. There are even severe withdrawal symptoms (like delirium tremens – the DTs) when you suddenly go without it.

DTs are horrible. They involve mental symptoms (like seeing frightening things that are not there), and physical symptoms, like nausea, vomiting and hot and cold sweats and shivers. If you experience some of these symptoms when you go a day without alcohol, then you are dependent on this powerful drug. If you continue with alcohol at your usual levels, it will be quietly, unknown to you, wrecking your stomach, liver and brain. Long periods of drinking too much produce stomach and pancreas cancer, liver failure (often with cirrhosis) and a severe brain problem known as alcoholic encephalopathy. In this last disease, you lose intellect and short-term memory, keep repeating sentences that you forget you have just uttered, and develop a form of epilepsy. Your normal life has gone, and can only be retrieved if you become teetotal. You may also need a liver transplant.

Obviously, if you are drinking too much, you will already know the social consequences. You have probably argued with your partner or spouse, or close family and friends (if you have any friends left). You are probably in debt. You may be losing your job and be in trouble with the police. You may already have caused an accident for which, when sober, you feel guilty and ashamed.

All this is part of your depression, and you may not be able to see how you can alter things. You may feel that you are in too deep, and that it is hopeless trying to reform. Yet that's not true. In my years as a general practitioner, I have seen several people whose drinking has led them to the edge of the abyss. They had lost family and friends, had even been in jail, and had made several attempts at suicide. When they finally stopped drinking, they became normal, responsible, reasonably happy citizens again. Only then could they sort out the reason for their drinking. In each case, the cause was an underlying depression, and when this was faced and treated, they became well. If you recognize yourself in these last few paragraphs, do take note. You can do it, too.

So how much alcohol are you drinking? Go over each day in the last few weeks. Put down, very honestly, the amount of each alcoholic drink you have swallowed. Count half a pint of beer, a small measure of spirits, or a small glass of wine as one unit. That means that the sort of drink you pour out at home, or are given in other people's homes, is usually two or more units. If you are drinking more than three units (for a man) or more than two units (for a woman) each day, you are drinking too much. If you are drinking more than double these amounts, you are drinking so much that you are likely to have withdrawal symptoms (such as sleeplessness, irritability, sweating, nausea, headaches and even the DTs) when you stop suddenly.

Your aim should be to lower your intake to within the amounts that are acceptable and have been shown to cause no long-term harm. Better still, don't drink at all for at least two days a week, to give your liver, pancreas, stomach and brain a rest from it. Make up a plan, so that you drop your drinking gradually, by a few drinks per week, over several weeks. This slow fall in your alcohol intake is easier to tolerate than a sudden steep drop.

One way to ease the process of lowering your alcohol intake is to intersperse non-alcoholic drinks between alcoholic ones. Fruit juices may be too sweet for you, and be too fattening for your liking (although remember that many people are overweight from their drinking; alcohol also contains calories, though they are not always counted by dieters.) Instead, you could get to like drinks like a 'pink tonic' – a tonic water with just a few drops of Angostura bitters, naturally without the gin. Or a planter's without the 'punch'. That is half-and-half ginger ale and ginger beer with again some Angostura to give it a bitter taste and a little 'kick' that you could persuade yourself to believe is alcohol!

When you are reducing your alcohol levels, do it under the supervision of someone who knows how to do it. In your family doctor team there will be someone who can guide you through the first few weeks. You can try Alcoholics Anonymous (AA), but do understand that many AA members believe that it's best to drink no alcohol at all, and that the best way to achieve that is to go 'cold turkey' and stop immediately. If you have been drinking a lot, this will bring on many of the withdrawal symptoms described above, and even heighten your depression. Although I'm a strong supporter of AA, I don't feel that this is the right approach for a depressive who drinks too much. You must aim at a goal you can realistically achieve, and suddenly stopping drinking after years of alcohol abuse is extremely difficult, and sometimes dangerous. It has even been known to precipitate people into attempting suicide – and that's the very thing we want to avoid.

I can add a few practical points about lowering your drink intake. Do be clear about how you want to do it. If you usually buy a six-pack at your local supermarket, just buy two cans at a time instead. It may mean you will have to go to the shops more often, but the extra trouble you have to take will reinforce your determination to keep to your target. When buying wine, buy one or two bottles at a time. Don't go for the '3 for fl10' approach, so that you are buying more than you really need just to save money. It's odds on you will drink them sooner than you planned, rather than allow them to remain on your wine rack.

At a restaurant for dinner, have a jug of water at the table and drink a glass of it between each glass of wine. That has the double effect of diluting the alcohol and filling you up so you feel less thirsty. And if you are debating ordering a second bottle, come down on the side of 'no, I've had enough'. Remember that two glasses are your maximum for the day if you are a woman, and three if you are a man. Many restaurants are generous with their measures – each glass may be the equivalent of one and a half or two standard measures.

If you are invited out to a party, say, where you know there will be plenty to drink, try to stick to your planned quota for that night. Remember that the first two drinks may weaken your resolve to keep down your consumption. That thought that comes with the alcohol 'rush', of 'I'll just treat myself tonight and let go' is a dangerous one. You won't be the first person to plan on having two drinks and finish up having ten. No matter how good you feel while you are doing it, the next morning you will be racked with guilt – and, most likely, with a hangover. Yet you can turn that to your advantage. Look on it as a lesson not to be repeated. Your plan is a long-term one, and you can still bring down your drinking levels slowly and surely over the subsequent weeks. Don't see that one night's lapse as a failure or become guilty about it – these are the negative thoughts that you promised to banish in a previous chapter. Instead, see the experience as a challenge that you can overcome and not repeat.

Once you get down to your target drinking level and have stuck to it for some weeks, savour the fact that you have achieved something that will stand you in good stead for the rest of your life. Be proud of yourself, and that, too, will help lift your depression even further. You have initiated a virtuous spiral upwards, in that by reducing your drinking you have become less depressed. That has improved your self-esteem, which in turn will lift your depression further. Keeping to your planned drinking habits will give an added boost to your self-esteem. It will also vastly improve your relationships with friends and family, and your efficiency and satisfaction at work. Your depression may well melt away alongside your reducing alcohol consumption.

In 2003, any discussion on alcohol must be linked to a discussion of the use of illicit drugs. When soap stars fall to their deaths from fourth-floor windows after reportedly binging on alcohol and cocaine, it must be obvious that drug abuse and depression don't mix. Drugs have an undeserved reputation for being 'uppers' (that brighten mood), rather than the 'downers' that they really are. That goes just as much for cannabis as for cocaine and heroin and its substitutes. If you are prone to depression, any of these 'recreational' drugs (a name to which I object, as it seems to confer some sort of respectability on them) will only in the long run make the depression worse.

Long-term use of such drugs can only complicate depressive illness, particularly if it is severe. It is especially a problem in people who use them on top of taking modern antidepressant drugs. There have not been enough studies to clarify how illicit drugs and prescribed drugs interact, and until such studies are published it is wise not to combine the two. My own experience of looking after many young men and women who have taken cannabis, cocaine and heroin leads me to believe that they are always destructive and never life-enhancing. I realize that this is anecdotal evidence, but the young adult drug abusers in the area in which I work, the south west of Scotland, have all, without exception, been badly damaged, physically and mentally, by their habits.

If you are taking illicit drugs, please seek help. Your family doctor will put you in touch with your local support groups. Please don't hesitate: it may save your life.

Chapter Fourteen

Sorting out Your Sleep

Sleep is almost always a problem if you are depressed. The classical description of sleep disturbance in depression is early-morning waking. You get to sleep normally, but wake in the early hours – any time between 2 a.m. and 6 a.m. – and can't get back to sleep again. You lie awake, mulling over your problems and depressing yourself further because you see no solution to them, and at that time in the morning you can do nothing constructive about them. Also at that time in the morning your brain is in no shape to reason and solve problems. You are only half awake, and you may well be in that peculiar state we have all experienced of being half awake and half dreaming. That's no time to be taking decisions.

When doctors hear that story, they put down 'depression' as the first probable diagnosis on your case sheet. You are depressed unless proven otherwise.

However, this type of sleep disturbance isn't the whole story in depression. Many people who are depressed find that they can't get to sleep in the first place. They toss and turn and can't drop off, even though they have felt tired all day. They are desperate to fall asleep, yet they can't.

It's difficult to define when occasional sleeplessness becomes clinical insomnia, a condition that begins to interfere with your quality of life. It is probably enough to agree that people who find that lack of sleep is a big thing in their lives have a problem that needs to be faced.

How much sleep we actually need to be physically healthy varies from person to person. A few people (famously, Mrs Thatcher again) seem to need only around four to five hours a night. Most of us need at least seven to wake fresh every morning: some need eight or more. We need less sleep as we grow older, so that by the time we reach 70 we need two or three hours less sleep each night than we did as young adults.

So if we have problems sleeping, what can we do about them? The first priority is to make your bedroom environment the right one for inducing sleep. As we get ready for sleep, we need to be able to relax and forget about the worries and woes, or the excitements, of our everyday life. So the first rule is to make the bedroom a quiet place that can be darkened enough to prevent light from interfering with the initial process of shutting down your active brain.

That means no television in the bedroom. Nor should you read or work. What is allowed is a 'snooze' radio, which you can switch on to music to your taste that allows you to listen with eyes closed, in the dark, and to doze off. It then switches itself off after you have fallen asleep. For some people, that works well. Others need absolute quiet. My own preference is for the radio to be on, as that can distract you from mulling over all the worrying and depressing things that seem to have happened to you in the previous day.

However, the preparation for sleeping starts before the bedroom. Don't eat much in the two to three hours before going to bed, as the process of digestion can keep you awake. If you are on a fitness programme – a good thing for anyone with depression – then finish the day's physical activities in the early evening, so that your body has completely recovered from its exertions before you think of sleeping. Sex, you will be pleased to note, is an exception to this. Most people feel sleepier after making love, and drop off more easily on nights when they do so than on nights when they don't.

Of course, your bed must be comfortable, with a good mattress that isn't sagging and lumpy. A new mattress every few years is a good help to sleep. If you haven't changed your mattress in the last ten years or so, then you are probably not as comfortable as you should be.

All the above are recommendations for good sleeping conditions for non-depressed people. If you are depressed, you have extra obstacles to overcome. Many people with the combination of depression and anxiety (which, as I mentioned before, is a common combination of problems in people seeing their family doctors) can't get off to sleep in the first place. They then wake up several times during the night, eventually waking too early in the morning and lying awake until it is time to get up.

The main cause of such a sleep pattern is anxiety. You can't stop worrying about what has happened during the day, or what is happening tomorrow, or a problem that has been present for some time. Worry wakens you up because it causes you to produce excess adrenaline – which speeds up the heart and alerts the brain – the very opposite of what happens when you are beginning to sleep. You may even feel your heart beating in your chest or your ears, you become a little restless, your stomach can't stop rumbling and you are a little nauseated. Your muscles may be tense and you can't find a position in which you can comfortably 'drop off'.

So try positively not to think about the day's worries. Leave them outside the bedroom door. The radio will help to distract you, as will a kind, sensitive and loving partner. Whether you just cuddle together or make love doesn't matter – the close contact and contentment make for a good start to your night's sleep.

It's important, too, to avoid stimulants before sleeping. Caffeine is the most obvious: we all know that caffeine-containing drinks can keep us awake. Not everyone knows that there is caffeine in drinks other than coffee. Hot chocolate, colas, tea and many herbal teas also contain enough caffeine to make a difference. If you are drinking five or more cups of coffee or tea in a day then the caffeine levels in your blood and brain are high enough to keep you awake for the first part of the night. So either don't drink them after the early evening or drink caffeine-free drinks instead. Drinks like Horlicks or Ovaltine have been shown to help people to get off to sleep, but they seem to have fallen out of fashion.

Don't smoke before bedtime, either. Nicotine is at least as powerful a brain stimulant as caffeine (and in the long term much more dangerous). Smoking in bed, of course, should be taboo. If you do drop off with a lighted cigarette in your fingers or mouth you have a fair chance of not waking up at all. In my time as a doctor I've been called to three separate incidents in which people died because they smoked in bed. All three of them had been drinking alcohol, too. The combination of being slightly drunk, and therefore clumsy with matches and lighted cigarettes, and being in bed, unable to get out of it quickly, is lethal.

Even if you don't smoke, an alcoholic drink before bedtime may send you to sleep (because you are under the influence), but will waken you up in the small hours of the morning as the brain is stimulated by the falling levels of alcohol within it.

Alcohol is a sedative. That is, it sends you to sleep. However, the effect lasts only a few hours (depending on the dose you have drunk) and then the brain undergoes a 'rebound'. As the alcohol is removed from the brain it becomes over-stimulated and you suddenly become wide awake. That usually happens between three and five in the morning, after which you will be wide awake for some hours. This is depressing in itself, but the depression is compounded by the fact that you will then feel really sleepy again at around 11 a.m., when you are supposed to be at work. It doesn't do your morale and self-esteem any good to be found asleep at your desk by your colleagues or boss.

Of course, the worst thing you can do if you aren't sleeping properly is to worry about it. Then you are adding to your problems, rather than solving them. Many people with insomnia worry that their lack of sleep will damage them in some way. For example, they feel that if they don't sleep for eight hours a night, the quality of their work, or their ability to look after their family, will suffer. This is a form of the unhelpful 'extreme' thinking that was described earlier. You need to deal with such thoughts appropriately, by banishing them. You can help yourself by relaxing before bed. Lying on the floor on your back, with head slightly raised and resting on a hard book (two telephone directories are ideal) and eyes shut, listening to soothing music, while focussing on relaxing each group of muscles in turn, is an excellent way to prepare for bed.

There are other approaches. I had an aunt with insomnia. She hardly slept through any night of her 90-plus years. She solved her problem by listening to the night-time radio and by reading books. She had come to terms with her sleeplessness and finally decided to make the most of it by keeping herself entertained. She must have come close to the world record for the total number of hours she spent conscious over her lifetime. She came to absolutely no harm, intellectually or physically, because of her lack of sleep. She isn't unusual. Studies of people who sleep very little have shown that they can carry out their daily duties perfectly adequately on as little as four and a half hours of sleep a night, and not feel unduly tired.

However, my sleepless aunt was not depressed. If you are not sleeping because you are depressed, you don't want to spend the night hours awake and worrying about yourself. You will feel happier if you can have regular oblivion every night. So to help you achieve that, and apart from the advice above, I can add a few tips that I have found useful over the years in helping people with insomnia, whether or not they were depressed.

One is to set a time for going to bed every night, say between 10 p.m. and midnight. Another, just as important, is to set a time to get up every morning, say between 8 a.m. and 9 a.m. Lying in bed too long can also disturb your wakefulness and your mood. It's good to be active in the morning: that's when your body clock tells you to be up and about and alert. If you can't get off to sleep, get up and do something around the house until you feel tired. As soon as you do so, get to bed. Respond to the signal as soon as you can and you should 'drop off'.

Taking naps during the day is controversial. Some experts hold that they do no harm and don't disturb night-time sleep. I'm not so sure about that. Professor Chris Williams, whose book on Overcoming Depression I have mentioned several times, is quite definite that daytime napping does interfere with sleeping at night. He prefers his patients not to nap during the day, so that they are better prepared to sleep at night.

A final thought about sleep. Many people who think they have insomnia don't have it at all. In Britain we have had excellent sleep research laboratories in Edinburgh, Loughborough and other universities, where volunteers with normal and other sleep patterns have been studied at length. One surprising result of the research was that many people who think they don't sleep well actually have near-normal sleep patterns. Measurements of their brainwave patterns (electroencephalography, or EEG) show that when they think they are awake they are actually asleep, but dreaming they are awake!

So don't get angry with your doctor if it is suggested to you that perhaps you sleep enough and that you don't need any pills to help you to sleep. Doctors are wary of prescribing sleeping pills for any long period, for lots of reasons. One is that few people actually need them, if they can organize their sleeping arrangements properly. Another is that they may work for a while, but their effect wears off, leaving the person dependent on them, but still sleeping badly. The guidelines for British doctors wishing to help people sleep with pills state that sleeping pills should not be taken on more than ten nights in any month, and preferably never on consecutive nights. This may help avoid dependence and allow the pill to keep its action and work more effectively.

Most important for people who are both sleepless and depressed, some sleeping pills and capsules may make you more depressed and give a slight 'hangover' during the morning after. Many doctors feel it is better to treat the depression as the primary illness, and that, as it improves, so will the sleeplessness. I agree with that.

Chapter Fifteen

Bringing it all Together

As a football pundit might put it, this has been a book of two halves. The first explained why people get depressed and the reasoning behind the drug treatment that almost everyone with depression is offered today. The second is more of a self-understanding and self-help manual, based on the techniques used by experts in cognitive behaviour therapy. It is vital to understand that the two halves are complementary, and not in opposition to each other. They are to be used together: that way you will have your best chance of throwing off your depression. Drugs and advice can be given by your doctors, but you have your part to play in understanding your depression and behaving appropriately.

So please use this book as a reference book for all the problems related to depression. If you recognize some of your symptoms in its pages, look at the relevant section and try to put into practice what it says about them. You will not always succeed, but keep trying. The more you learn about your depressive illness, the better the chance you have of overcoming it. A good tip is to ask your closest friend or relative to read it with you, so that he or she can support you through the difficult periods that are bound to arise from time to time. If you both work together on improving your understanding and altering your thoughts and behaviour accordingly, you have a much better chance of success.

Always keep in mind that you won't have your depression forever. Depression is a 'cyclical' illness, in that it comes and goes. For years you may be free of it, then it hits, out of the blue, and you feel you are falling into a black hole. Most people with the illness know when it is switching on. That's the time to seek urgent help. Don't delay: the sooner you can be treated the faster the depression will be lifted. That's why you should accept both types of treatment – drugs and cognitive behaviour therapy. Together they should bring you through this episode of depression with the minimum of misery.

As for taking antidepressant drugs, it is probably appropriate here to reproduce a few questions about them that every general practitioner hears, mainly from people worried about taking modern pharmaceuticals. All the news reports about new drugs seem to be antagonistic to them, and it is no wonder that so many people mistrust them. Yet they have made a huge difference to the vast majority of people with severe depression – one that ranks alongside the discovery of antibiotics for infection or insulin for diabetes – in the last 50 years. For doctors like myself who have watched the transition from the older drugs to the newer ones, they have been close to miraculous in their improved effects and relative lack of side effects. So here are my answers to the most commonly asked questions.

Q I've been taking an antidepressant for a week now, and I still don'tfeel any better. Should I stop it?

A No. Because antidepressants have to work on brain chemistry, it takes two weeks or more before you feel a rise in mood, and that rise continues to improve you for a further two to four weeks. So you won't feel the maximum benefit for around six weeks after starting the drug. You should continue to feel the benefit after that, in the long term.

Q How long do you expect me to be taking the antidepressant for? Can I stop it once I feel better?

A Most courses of antidepressants last at least six months, and many doctors prefer not to stop them until they have been taken constantly for two years. Please don't stop your treatment early without discussing it first with the doctor who prescribed it. If you do, you may have a 'rebound', a sudden deepening of your depression.

Q The leaflet with my prescription describes a whole host of side effects, some of which are frightening. How can I possibly take such a dangerous medicine?

A Product leaflets must, by law, mention all the side effects that have been reported by patients using the drug or by doctors pre-scribing it. However, for the newer antidepressants, the number of side effects is very low and they are usually tolerable. Most appear within the first few weeks of taking them and can be reversed either by lowering the drug dose or by changing to another drug with a different action. See the relevant section of this book for more details. The benefits of antidepressant drugs far outweigh their side effects, but please discuss them with your doctor if you have any doubts about your drug.

Q   Can I become addicted to my antidepressant?
A   No. Antidepressant drugs are not addictive. In this they are not like tranquillizers, some painkillers, sleeping tablets, tobacco or illicit drugs.

Q   If I'm feeling particularly low, can I increase the dose of my anti-depressant?
A   Absolutely not. Your dose is tailored to you and increasing it will not be more effective in raising your mood. If your depression is deepening or not responding to your drug, you should seek help from your prescribing doctor or the primary healthcare team member who knows you best. Do not alter your dose.

Q   If I miss a dose, should I take an extra one?
A   No. Antidepressant tablets work on a long-term basis. Missing one tablet will make little difference. Missing a lot of them over many days will be like lowering your dose or stopping the treatment, and that can lead to a return of your depression. It's best to mark out a particular time every day for taking your tablet (most are once daily nowadays), and be sure to take it at that time. Wristwatches that 'ping' at a pre-set time are ideal as reminders to take the tablet.

One last comment. Overcoming depression is, for anyone who has experienced this serious illness, a triumph. It gives freedom and a feeling of relief and enjoyment in life that can only be appreciated fully by someone who has been through it personally. So once you are back to normal, rejoice in it.

But be vigilant against its return. Remember that it may return in the future, and be prepared to ask for advice about it early in its next appearance. If you learn the early signs, you can get help before it really takes hold, and that can mean shortening the length of the episode and reducing its severity. Different people find that different aspects of their depression are prominent in these early stages. So take your choice from this list. You will surely recognize these feelings from your own experience.

I'm starting to think negatively again, looking on the black side and ignoring the good things.

I'm feeling low and unemotional, as if I don't care about anything.

I've stopped going out with friends and family. I don't enjoy their company any more. I'd rather be by myself.

I'm getting lazy and inactive. I'm getting up later than I used to, and want to lie in every morning.

I've got huge problems, and can't seem to be able to solve them. I can't even find the initiative to begin to solve them – I just want to hide away from them, and hope they will go away.

I keep thinking that others are judging me.

I've fallen back into the habit of trying to read other people's minds.

I've begun to drink a bit more.

I'm not doing well at work – I'm not as efficient or as effective as I was.

I'm getting stressed and nervy, and don't know how to deal with it.

I'm losing my self-confidence and self-esteem.

Do you recognize any or all of these statements? If they describe how you are feeling at this moment, please get help. You need it, and it is available. All you need to do is to make that appointment you know you should have made some time ago.

Bibliography

Williams, Professor Chris, *Overcoming Depression: A Five Areas Approach* (Arnold, 2001)

Stahl, Professor Stephen M., *Essential Psychopharmacology of Depression and Bipolar Disorder* (Cambridge University Press, 2000)

Mayer-Gross, Professor Willi, Slater, Professor Eliot and Roth, Professor Martin, *Clinical Psychiatry* (Cassell, 1960)

Index